You Have A College Degree, Now What?

You Have A College Degree, Now What?

Michael Esola
Wesley Jones

EJ Consulting

You Have A College Degree, Now What?

Copyright © 2010 by EJ Consulting
First Edition

ISBN: 978-0-578-04404-0

Printed in the United States of America

For more information regarding future titles and consulting services, please visit www.ejconsultingllc.com

CONTENTS

Acknowledgments

Many people helped to shape the development of this book including business colleagues, students, college professors, and the support of family and friends.

Special thanks to Alan and Darlene Esola, Tony and Karen Hoover, Carol Esola, Vidal Zuniga, Zac Christensen, O. Lee Mincey, Megan Laurie, Jennifer Esola, Joe McLoughlin, Jeff Habeeb, Scott Washington, Pedro Rodrigues, Jen Felix, Andreas Wolf, and Jeff Riddle.

A very special thanks to Inez Brasesco for showing us that you can truly do what you want in life.

Introduction

It was once thought that having a college degree was a great and noble achievement. In today's high paced and competitive world, it now seems that a master's degree is the equivalent of a bachelor's degree, and a bachelor's degree is now the equivalent of an associate's degree from yesteryear. Individuals with advanced degrees are often the brunt of jokes and, in some cases, struggle to become financially successful. One probably does not have to search too far to locate a hard working employee who has a college degree just struggling to earn minimum wage. In some cases, some of those degree-holding employees work in an unpaid internship just to earn a shot at an entry level position.

The following words of wisdom and reality are not meant in any way to demean or belittle the accomplishments of individuals who have worked hard to achieve such academic endeavors. After all, I would be belittling myself, and the fact is I am proud of earning my master's degree, bachelor's degree and associate's degree. It is time to answer the age-old question of, what does one do once one has earned a college degree?

Work on my undergraduate degree concluded in 2004, and my sights on an advanced degree were clear because everyone I knew was getting a bachelor's degree. It seemed that anyone could purchase a degree of his or her own. With that said, work on my own master's degree began in January, 2005. It was at that time that I worked my way toward what would eventually become a Master of Arts Degree in Sport Management.

I am constantly asked why I chose Sport Management. Quite frankly, it is because MBA degrees are very popular and common these days. After all, I could have easily gone online and earned an MBA while wearing my pajamas and drinking a glass of wine. I wanted something similar to an MBA, but more specific to an industry.

It has often been said that working in the sport world is almost as hard as trying to break into Hollywood. This is true, and I am still working on that one, too. So, naturally, I thought that having a master's degree in this accepted field would only enhance my chances of officially breaking into the ultra-competitive business world of sports and possibly entertainment. As I would soon learn, there are supporters on both sides of this argument.

My master's degree revolved around classes which were designed to prepare students for a career in the sport world. Instead, what the courses appeared to be was busy work which only vaguely prepared students for what each of my colleagues and I strived for: knowledge, success, and money in a distinguished industry. Busy work, which came at a very high financial cost, ultimately, led many of my colleagues to believe that they did not get a good return on investment for their money. Either way, my return on investment has resulted in a better understanding of what happens when one does, in fact, earn a college degree.

1

Discover What You Want

I encourage you to take a step back and analyze what everything means to you. Put this book down for a moment and think about what you want in life. What makes you happy? What type of career will enable you to jump out of bed in the morning with excitement? What will provide you with a work/life balance? Above all else, what are your dreams and aspirations, both short term and long term? After taking a moment to think about what you want, take a look around and see what it is all about.

Once I completed my graduate degree, I began the task of having informational meetings with various sport and entertainment industry leaders. While meeting with one particular athletic director to discuss the possibility of earning a Doctorate in Education, I learned a very valuable lesson. He said to me,

"Take a look around; this is what it's all about. I know the job of athletic director can seem sexy and attractive, but the truth of the matter is this is what it entails: me, my computer, and my quiet office. This is the part of the job that no one sees." Once I heard these words, I began to evaluate what things meant to me. I realized that in my own quest to become a Division I Director of Athletics, I had forgotten to find the true message. The message that I found was that each day I felt as if it was just me, my computer, my cell phone, and my office. I was all alone, and it was up to me to make things happen.

After having a better understanding of what I was trying to accomplish in life, I began to see things clearer. I could understand exactly what I needed to do and the process that would take me there. The process of how to actually get somewhere is something which should be taken into account. It should not be overlooked and can allow an individual to see the entire picture he or she is trying to depict. Having vision and being a visionary is one of the ways to accomplish great feats and is an essential first step in reaching dreams and goals.

People who are lost and confused have no sense of what their own path looks like. For one reason or another they have become sidetracked and may never return to their path. If one becomes sidetracked, it is never too late to get back on track headed down one's correct path. If anyone ever tells you that it is too late, these are words of pure lies. It is never too late, and it is important to understand this.

One needs to be able to formulate ideas regarding what lies ahead in one's life. I still have many large ideas circulating in my head. The difference between now and when I was in my youth is that I now have a good idea of what it will take to execute these certain ideas. My visualization of the process now is far greater than it was in my youth. When I was younger, I would only concentrate on the idea. Now I have a greater understanding of what the entire process will look like. The process is exactly the key element to executing the idea or dream. Many only dream the dream and do not know much about the hardships or sacrifices it will take to execute it.

Clarity while executing ideas is extremely important. Often times the only thing clear about an idea is the actual idea itself. The process of how to actually get there is often more important than the idea. It is this process of how to get there that will determine if that idea will be reality or simply just an idea. It is important to understand the complexity and dynamics of one's ideas and dreams. This will help one to figure out and prepare for the setbacks and obstacles to be faced. Having an idea of what one's path is beginning to look like and what it will take to continue traveling down it will make success all that much easier.

YOU HAVE A COLLEGE DEGREE, NOW WHAT?

My own reasons for not being satisfied with my 9-5 job revolved around several different issues. The first was that of my co-workers. Some of these individuals were the type of people who were looking for handouts. It was extremely frustrating, as I was trying to take the small steps toward doing something big, and others with whom I worked were just taking large steps toward something small. These negative individuals motivated me to make sure that I would never end up like them, simply waiting around for the next opportunity. This is a dangerous approach to take because an individual may wait a lifetime for an opportunity that is not coming.

The second issue that discouraged me from my day job did not revolve around lack of pay. Money, to me, would soon become irrelevant. It was the simple fact that no one will ever pay you what you are worth, unless you are lucky enough to find yourself on the Fortune 500 list. My complaint about my day job was that it did not motivate me. I did not spring out of bed in the morning wanting to go to work, and this was a thought that would often times sicken me. I knew that I could not go about the rest of my life working for someone else on a typical nine to five job. I simply would not survive.

One thing that I learned while being frustrated with my day job was that most of us have the entrepreneurial spirit within us. Some of us have ideas and dreams, but we seem to always tuck them away for a better time. There will never be a good time because something will always be in the way. If one has dreams and goals, then the time to act is the present. The time to strike is now, not tomorrow, and certainly not five years from now.

Too many people in life put off ideas or dreams about which they are passionate. It is easy to get caught up in the everyday concerns of life and soon lose track of time. Time is of the essence when we are not guaranteed a tomorrow. One must act now if one is truly to execute one's goals and dreams.

Throughout my life I have seen others, including myself from time-to-time, procrastinate in achieving certain things. This may be a result of a multitude of issues. The first issue would be time management. It is true that some people lack spare time. There are those individuals who claim to be busy, but they are really not. They often spend a good part of their day wasting time and not making the minutes and hours count.

The next type of procrastinating comes from holding on to a dream or belief. I have seen many individuals hold on to a dream while not executing it. I have also been guilty of this from time-to-time. I feel that it is because if you have a dream, you do not want to execute that dream only to see it fail. It seems that many do not execute because they are afraid of that dream coming to a crashing end.

I have friends who have written superb screenplays but never follow through submitting them to the appropriate people. I do not believe that they are discouraged by the tough uphill battle involved to get a screenplay accepted in Hollywood, but it is more of the fear that their dream could come to a disappointing end. However, if they never act, they always maintain that dream. They simply put off executing, always saying that they are too busy or the timing is not right. As I learned early on, there is never the correct time for anything.

Heading down the correct path for me has always revolved around following my dreams and ideas. To me, as long as I maintained a good work ethic toward executing my goals and dreams, then I was always positive that I was on the correct work path. After earning my graduate degree, I began to see that this was a time of uncertainty for some of my colleagues and friends. They began to waiver and appeared unsure as to what it was that they were exactly trying to accomplish. Some of them are still doing this today and will do so until the day they die. It is okay from time-to-time to be confused. Life is very confusing. Life is made easier and more meaningful, however, when you have dreams and goals for which you are always striving.

~

Finding what it is all about will require deep soul searching. One of the biggest questions you should ask yourself is if you have what it takes to chase your dreams and goals? If the answer to this is yes, then there is no reason you should not be able to do something if you set your mind to it. Do not let anyone get in your way. Dreams are sacred, and no one should ever insult someone else's dreams. They are what make us all unique and different.

The key is to take your dream from the dream stage to the doing stage. It is fair to say that everyone has dreams, but not everyone understands what they are all about. Few realize what it will, in fact, take to reach that dream. I encourage all to keep dreaming because it is what makes life great. However, it is important to understand the steps necessary to execute that dream, and that key first step is to discover what you want and lay out the blueprint of how to get it.

It is up to each individual to determine what the correct path is. What is right for one person might not be right for another. The same can also be said for close friends and family. Your family and close friends will always want what is best for you, and they may even try to dissuade you from following certain passions. It is important to do what you want to do. Failure to do so will result in doubts and regrets later on in life. There is nothing worse than looking back and having regrets on actions that you wish you took.

2

Survival of the Most Persistent

Are some dreams and goals in life simply unattainable? Is it possible for an individual to have set the bar too high in life? Should you just settle for the $50,000 a year job? I believe the answers to these questions will differ depending upon whom you ask. There are those who will tell you that you truly cannot do everything you want in life. There are certain people who are made to be at the top, and the remainder of society simply gets by at the bottom. I am here to tell you that this statement and belief is completely and utterly false.

After earning my graduate degree, I realized how important the concept of persistence is in life. The word persistent can mean different things to different people. Persistence might include resiliency, determination, motivation, and effort. Do you have big goals and aspirations in life? If the answer is yes, then the word persistent will play a monumental part in your road to success. No matter what age you might be, big goals and aspirations are achievable because nothing is impossible if you are the most persistent.

Many people in life view successful people as simply successful. While it may be true that some have had extraordinary breaks of luck along the way or certain competitive advantages, I firmly believe that most were simply more persistent than everyone else.

For many people in life, it is often human nature to quit. Quitting is a fact of life. Quitting is easy to do. Let's look at the stock market to demonstrate the idea of quitting. Successful investors will be quick to tell you that downturns in the market are opportunities for a select few. For the majority these downturns represent negative situations, but there are always those investors who will capitalize on the negative situation. The same can be said for quitting and being persistent. Quitting allows the persistent ones to succeed. It is almost as if the quitters in the world are valuable to the persistent ones because the persistent ones will be there to outlast everyone else.

~

Who has the answers, and where are they hidden? This is not the million dollar question, rather the billion dollar question. Highly successful people know how to enact certain strategies such as launching a massive company against a steady chorus of nay sayers, and they most certainly will not tell. They have the answers, and they will not give them to the rest of us. How then do we go about obtaining some of the knowledge that they have acquired? There are numerous answers to this question, but one answer that sits far above the rest is that of persistency. Without persistency one will not get very far in life. The best business plan and business model can be in place, but without persistency that business will most likely not even get off to a start.

Life is constantly weeding out people. Certain resumes rise to the top of the pile while others are discarded, many proceed onward while others quit, and some will make it in life while others will not. There is always some process of elimination which is taking place to some degree or another.

The first day out of graduate school, I realized that in order to execute some of my goals and dreams in life, I would have to be the most persistent person on the face of the earth. I still believe this philosophy to this day. It is persistency that will, ultimately, get you over the hump of anything you want to do. It will give you the extra nudge that you will need. If you want to achieve something great, then being persistent is about as vital as oxygen.

SURVIVAL OF THE MOST PERSISTENT

Any great idea will undoubtedly have pitfalls and set-backs. The real key is to be the individual who keeps going despite the many negative setbacks which may come about. It all comes down to how badly someone wants something? Ideas and dreams are not easy, and they are not supposed to be easy. If ideas and dreams were easy to achieve, then everyone would be able to live out their fantasies. It all will come down to who is the most persistent. After you have discovered what you want, you must become the most persistent person ever in achieving what you want. Persistency is one of the few assets that is more valuable than gold or the most precious jewels. Acquire it and you just may achieve something in life that truly is out-of-this-world.

3

Personal Brand

Working on my own personal brand each and every day became a regular routine from the start of undergraduate school. I began to read every book related to ways of improving my own personal brand. One's personal brand can consist of everything from how one speaks to how one is dressed. One's personal brand is essentially a first impression to the people around you. First impressions are extremely important in our world, and if one does not give a great first impression, one's college degree may be nothing more than a piece of paper to hang on the wall.

Public speaking is a very important skill that must be mastered in order to achieve success. During the interview process, business presentation, or networking event, those around you do not care if you have a piece of paper that has a college degree written on it. They will be listening to how you speak.

My graduate classes touched upon the art of speaking in a better and more concise manner. The key to speaking better in public is to clean up your language at home, work and around friends. The basic premise is that in order to have supreme speaking skills, one must use them at all times of day, not just when speaking to a large group of people. Good speaking must be second nature. Eliminate words such as um, really, like, and you know. These, along with a host of other words, have contributed in some small way to the demise of the English language. There is nothing worse than listening to a colleague communicate information in a way that must contain an abundance of ums, likes and you knows. As a speaker, one must be aware of how often these filler words are used. Pretend they are curse words and exclude them from your vocabulary.

Having stuttered since a young age, I often found it hard to express what I was feeling as a result of my speech problems. After college I took it upon myself to try as best I could to speak proper English. This is a task which is easier said than done. The stutter has always been there and seemed to always raise its nasty head in the worst of times, such as public speaking and presenting projects to various classes in college. I now feel as if

I know how to control the embarrassing stuttering and other nervous speaking jitters.

It is important to be able to replicate the feelings and anxiety that one might feel while giving a public address. I was always able to replicate exactly how I would feel speaking in front of a group of people. Therefore, I had the added luxury of dealing with the jitters and stuttering before actually giving the speech. It is also important to notice what triggers one to stutter, if that is indeed one's problem, such as it was with me.

The next time you listen to someone in the public forum giving a speech, pay attention to the language he or she uses. You will be surprised that when you know which words you need to eliminate from your vocabulary, you might even be shocked to hear very prominent people using them. Many people often use language that is not proper, thereby causing one to wonder how in the world they ever got to where they are today.

I remember giving many speeches while in public and not being able to hear myself speak. It is important that you are able to hear yourself to some degree so you can avoid certain words. Individuals who do not hear themselves speaking often use the exact same words over and over. These types of speeches can be painful to watch and listen to because it is like watching the collapse of someone right before your eyes. Better speaking starts with being able to address the words that should be obliterated from one's vocabulary. It is hard to break habits that we have had throughout our entire lives, but once again if you value it, you will do it. Nothing comes easy, and for most this one will not either.

A great public speaker can motivate in ways unimaginable. Reaching this level takes time and effort. I have found that even if you are using incorrect words but at least catching yourself in the act of using them, you are, ultimately, on your way to ridding yourself of these words. Many times I have caught myself in the act of using words I am trying to eliminate. This is the first stage because it means that I am aware of how I sound.

The next time you speak try to hone in on how you sound. Can you hear yourself speaking and what do you sound like? Often times I would call myself on my cell phone and leave a message just as I would for someone else. The reason for this is so I could gauge how I sounded over the telephone. The same principle exists for athletes who watch themselves on film. They want to see what they look like and how they perform.

I remember when I first saw my golf swing on camera. I had a certain image in my head of what I looked like and was shocked when my mental image did not fit what I looked like on film. It was extremely beneficial for me because I was able to correct the flaws once I realized what I looked like.

The same can be said for public speaking. Film your speeches and mock interviews so that you can review what is effective and what needs improving. While most people do not like hearing and seeing themselves on camera or audio, it is important to hear and see yourself if you are to correct your flaws. Smart people want to look at their flaws and learn from them while the so-called people who claim to know everything feel as if they have nothing to learn. Open your eyes and ears up to what you really sound like. This is truly the first and most critical step in cleaning up one's language and eventually delivering a great speech.

An individual can be extremely intelligent but have poor speaking skills. It is a possibility that he or she might come off as unintelligent as a result of these poor speaking skills. If an individual is of average or below average intelligence, but has superb speaking skills, it is possible for that individual to appear to be extremely intelligent. When we meet individuals for the first time, one of our first impressions of them will be the speaking skills they possess. Speaking can make or break a first impression, so this component of our personal brand highly depends on flawlessness.

People who struggle with speech have a hard time both socially and professionally. Again, if you struggle with speech or are using too many filler words such as um, like, and you know, then the time to improve should be immediately. At the very least, improving your command of speaking will most likely improve your overall character. You will begin to hold yourself in higher esteem than you might previously have done. If you want to be in the public eye or even ascend to higher levels of success, good speaking habits are a must.

~

Personal appearance is also about first impressions. One might think that this is a no brainer and an easy one to comprehend. Well, not exactly. I am amazed at how often someone will come into my office for an interview and look like they just crawled out of a ditch full of mud. Dress to impress. Dress for the job you want. Above all else, dress like you care about yourself.

In today's ever changing society, dress attire is only half the battle. It is also about how well you look. Are you fit? Being overweight signifies unhealthiness and laziness whereas being toned or fit represents a healthy and strong ability to achieve. If you cannot afford a gym membership, find the closest park and run or walk as much as possible. Fresh air will do the body good, too. The key here is to stay in shape because your appearance will help get you where you want to go, but just being healthy is important, too. If for any reason, whatsoever, stay in shape for yourself! Staying in shape is also a great way of feeling good when one wakes up in the morning, and it will provide more energy to help with reaching one's goals.

One area of fitness that is also overlooked is how it can help one maintain a rigorous yet disciplined schedule. Once again, I look to a close colleague of mine. He trains very hard in the weight room and also works on his cardio on a regular basis. The reason is so that he can be mentally fit and alert at all times throughout the day. Being physically fit allows one to stay both strong and healthy. We all know that work can, at times, beat you up no matter in which industry you are. The better shape you are in will, ultimately, allow you to last longer at work and recuperate faster. If you want to feel as if you will be strong to compete, then it is imperative to stay in the best of shape at all times.

Improving my fitness level allowed me to work off aggression and frustration. Many people who are out of shape do not know how good it feels to be in shape. It allows one to keep up a relentless pace. Everyone becomes sick and worn down from time to time, but being in better shape will make everyday living that much better.

Does it happen for most people? Not really. The trend in life is repeated in many individuals. I like to refer to this as the downward spiral. An example would be an individual who works twelve hour days. That individual now has no time for fitness or cooking well-balanced meals. He or she begins eating fast food or eating on the run, and now there is no time to exercise. Even worse is that fast food just sits in an unexercised body. This individual's personal brand suffers and a few years go by where that certain individual becomes thirty pounds overweight. Examples such as these have now become common in today's society, as there are record levels of obese people in America. This is a trend which is damaging to one's health and can have a major impact on one's personal brand if that person loses self control.

Making fitness and eating healthy a priority in one's life will accomplish many positive things. A person must convince him or herself that these issues are extremely important to well being and the longevity that one will either have or not have in the lifetime of health. The number one reason why individuals claim not to exercise is probably because of time. Most will say that they do not have any time. The problem lies in the fact that many do not put a high priority on exercise and fitness. It must be ingrained into someone's head that this is extremely important. If one does not maintain a good level of fitness and exercise, what will the quality of life be?

There is no doubt that we can all find extra time during the week. It basically comes down to what we put at the top of our priority list. Having a family and working full time will undoubtedly take up most of an individual's time, but it is still important to make exercise a priority. This is something which should not be taken lightly and cannot be stressed enough.

I have always enjoyed weightlifting. I would start with a good set of pushups and then move on over to weights. I have noticed that on weeks when I have not been able to get some weight work or physical fitness in, my mental attitude appeared to be slightly less. I am a firm believer that activities such as weightlifting and cardio-vascular exercises contribute to staying mentally sharp, and, in return, affect one's personal brand. At the end of a strong workout, one should feel good, as if that individual has accomplished something and becomes brand new.

~

Posture is a topic that is never really discussed when it comes to personal brand, and this should not be the case. I always found myself trying to improve my posture. My goal was to make it second nature. Once bad habits are learned in life, they are hard to break. It is also important to remember that anyone can break bad habits. It comes down to mental strength.

Are you strong enough mentally to sit up straight at meetings, in class, or during a big job interview? Posture is something which I cannot emphasize enough. It is something upon which every-one can always be working.

Many people can appear as if they are defeated or de-pressed just by holding a certain posture. Practicing good posture is just a matter of doing it and being conscious about it. It is all about thinking positive and looking positive.

~

Part of one's personal brand is presenting a positive im-age to those around you. No matter what situation you might be in, it is important to always act positively because it reflects your brand. There is never anything to gain from acting negatively. A negative outlook will rarely help one at all. Being a positive individual can have a positive effect on both the individual and the outside public.

It is fair to say that as people in the work world, we are always onstage or on public display. One never knows who may be watching or judging you for work or other areas. How some-one presents himself or herself to the public is something of extreme importance. Individuals need to constantly take pride in their appearance and value the way others see them. By doing so, it will make being professional in the work place that much easier. Individuals need to train themselves to display appropriate behavior. By accomplishing all of the above, it will make that next big meeting with a very important person that much more successful.

~

The way that I began to carry myself after college created a branded image associated with me. Everyone possesses an individual brand. From the way we are dressed to the way we are organized, we must look the part if we want success. The problem with many people is that they do not take pride in their brand. They can often be lazy, sloppy, and negative individuals. I have been around quite a few of these individuals in my lifetime. Most people are not aware that they are a brand that they have created. We have the power to either present a positive or negative brand. There simply is nothing to gain from presenting a negative brand to the public.

Smart and successful people know what their brand consists of at all times. Being able to improve one's personal brand is to realize that one is always on public display or onstage at all times. Once this is realized, it becomes increasingly easier to act upon that brand. Whether people want to admit it or not, everyone has traits that can be improved. People who claim to be perfect are simply blinded by their own ignorance. It is important not to be one of those individuals. Always be sure to strive for more with your personal brand.

PERSONAL BRAND

Each of us has a brand that changes from adolescence to adulthood. When we are a teenager, our brand is significantly different from when we are a young adult. It is our job to work on our brand as we go through different stages in life. It is often exciting to know that our personal brand will always be changing and evolving throughout our lives.

4

Time Management

Time is one of the most precious things we possess. Time can be more valuable than money. We can often get money back, but we cannot get time back. We, as humans, can financially bankrupt ourselves yet we still might be able to earn all of it back. However, if we throw ten years of our lives away, then we are left to suffer the consequences.

Use your time wisely and treat it like the precious commodity that it is. It is important to know how much free time you have during the day, and then make the most out of it. Time becomes an even more precious commodity when we begin to work full time and have family commitments. Americans spend a great deal of time working at their day jobs. This, therefore, places even more importance on the free time that is available at the end of the day.

~

It is important to maintain a clean work and living space. If you are going to be able to work at your maximum performance, you must have a clear mind. You need to be free of all unnecessary distractions. There is nothing more frustrating and distracting than working in a cluttered work space. While personal organization could be considered a personal brand component, I consider it a major component of one's time management. It can either make or break our time management skills, and it can reveal who we really are.

I have had two types of bosses; the one with the clean desk and the one with the cluttered desk. The boss with the clean desk has typically always been the better boss. Cleanliness and tidiness are often associated with a better work ethic.

It all comes down to a matter of cleanliness and what one exactly considers as neat and clean. I always take extreme pride in my work space, for it is where I hash out new ideas and work on existing ones. I consider my work space a place for innovation and dreams to be chased and achieved. I, therefore, take great pride in this place and always make sure that it is in order. Nothing is more frustrating than when my work space is out of order. It does not allow me to think clearly. It is as if there is always something at the back of my head distracting me. Clutter in the work space does nothing but clutter your thoughts and what potentially could be groundbreaking ideas; so keep your space clutter free.

It is highly recommended that you purchase a filing cabinet to organize all of your important documents and information. This will make finding and storing your documents much easier. You will be able to pull up important pieces of paper in seconds instead of having to fumble through piles of paperwork. This type of filing system will make you more efficient, and you will not waste valuable work time looking for documents.

I have seen the benefits firsthand of filing documents away properly. It is also important to note that once you receive a document, chances are one day you will have to pull it up again. It makes life so much easier if you can find it quickly and with ease.

Part of being organized is maintaining your resources efficiently. This includes keeping your email, voicemail, traditional mailbox, and other communication tools in order. Before the workday concludes, you should always empty out your email inbox. No, this does not mean deleting every message, but it does mean responding to every email and taking care of the necessary business. Whether you have forty or four hundred unanswered emails, it is essential that you take care of them before your day concludes. If you fail to do so, you can become disorganized, and the forty or four hundred could turn into eighty or eight hundred by the next day. Before you know it, your time management processes will become affected, and you will be labeled as the one who is the most unreliable and disorganized person in the organization. The same message can be true about voicemails and traditional mail. Do not put it off. Take care of it once you get it.

Keeping "To-Do" lists is probably the most efficient way of staying organized. Make a list at the end of the day of what needs to be completed the next day. Throughout the next day check off what you accomplish and, at the end of the day, make a new list. Do not forget to include the items that you did not complete. Always allow yourself enough time in the day for unexpected events, such as interruptions by your boss or extra long organizational meetings that often may not be organized efficiently.

Being organized does not mean cleaning your house during spring once a year. A clean and organized person will probably never have to participate in spring cleaning because that individual maintains a continual level of cleanliness and organization. It is difficult enough to be successful in this world, and the last thing I need is my desk to be a distraction because it is messy. You do not want your house to turn into a distraction because of how sloppy it is. Your house or living space should be a place where you can go to relax and get away from the clutter that exists in the world.

~

The number of people in the world who waste time must be astonishing. So many of my former colleagues have wasted their time day-in and day-out, and I was led to believe that the only way to achieve things was to master time management. When my time management skills improved, I, ultimately, found myself achieving more in a shorter period of time. If you are going to work on side projects and still continue to work a full time job, you must make certain that your time management skills are indeed excellent. It can be very challenging, and, at first, I struggled with the issue of working after I came home from work. Yet, it can be accomplished.

The key to using your time wisely is to start to condition yourself like an exercise routine. I began a routine that included coming home, cooking dinner, cleaning, making the next day's lunch, and then sitting down around 8 P.M. in the evening to begin my work. Each day it seemed as if I had around three hours to get some solid work done. Three hours is a great deal of time to get good work done, but I have seen firsthand that it can easily be squandered.

TIME MANAGEMENT

Modern day distractions such as television and the internet can make achieving work at night challenging. It is so tempting to turn on the television and sit in front of it. There is also nothing wrong with this because we all need to relax from time-to-time. I realized that if I was going to maintain a normal job and work on my projects outside of normal business hours, then, in a sense, I had to be very disciplined. Oftentimes I felt as if I were a machine, working all day and then pounding out another three hours of work at night. I did not like living like this way, but who else would do this work for me? No one was going to help me with my projects. Therefore, it fell on my shoulders to get it done. I knew of no other way to get my work done than the way which I enacted, and it required a strict routine of time management enforcements.

Deciding upon a game plan early on was critical to achieving results and completing projects. It took me some time before I realized that I could arrive home at night, work out for one hour, cook a meal, clean, make my lunch for the next day, and still have approximately three hours to achieve whatever I needed to do. It is also important to remember that a great deal of time can also be wasted in three hours. The choice is simply up to the individual. Are you going to make good use of your time, or are you going to squander it away like so many have and will continue to do?

Life is short, and the amount of time we have for working on our own projects is even shorter. I feel that working away from work has helped me to better understand the concept of time and how long it takes to accomplish one's goals. Most people fail to realize how long things take to do, and the idea that nothing happens overnight is very true. There are always examples that would disprove this theory, but, for the most part, it is accurate and represents reality to the fullest.

~

My college degrees offered me a new set of eyes with which to see the real world. They convinced me that I could achieve great things with my spare time. I reserved my spare time for reading, writing books, screenplays, and pitching and building business plans. I made sure to keep an arsenal of coals always going into the fire. I figured that the more things I had going on at once, the more likely I would be to succeed.

Success is not merely about being lucky. Success is about putting yourself in the correct position for lucky circumstances to occur. By working hard during my spare time, I was, hopefully, putting myself in this much coveted position.

I felt as if becoming successful would only be a matter of time for one simple reason. I started to thoroughly enjoy the entire process of working on all my projects. I also found myself working harder at my day job, knowing that all I wanted to do was come home and pick up where I left off.

This is also a key to becoming a better employee for someone else. Too often it appears to be the case in the business world that people are miserable at work because they have nothing that motivates them. Working on business plans and reading at night motivated me during my day job in ways that I never thought possible. My night work helped me develop as a business man. I felt as if I were on a perennial quest, searching for answers for the next great idea. Along with working on certain ideas, I always made sure that I was researching and reading material that would help me figure out what that next great idea was.

~

Reading everything you can get your hands on in your spare time will do nothing but improve your mental abilities. This was something of which I became very aware, and I routinely pushed to reach new heights with this mentality. Reading was something that I not only enjoyed but also used to help me become more competent in areas that I previously lacked.

Each time I finish reading a book, I feel as if I have just completed bench pressing three hundred pounds with my mind. The great thing about reading is that with each book one reads, one is exposed to certain words and issues, and these are often worthy of an entire book. The more I would read and learn, the more I would begin to realize how little I knew about the world I was trying so desperately to enter.

The more one reads, the more one will realize how important it is to be well read. Not only does reading help improve language and business acumen, but it also helps with one's personal development. Reading, therefore, is a skill that should always be cultivated.

I began to read various books each day during my lunchtime, which was spare time in itself. I liked knowing that I was achieving something other than just working for someone else during the daytime. I was taking steps that would help me in the future. It became both fun and relaxing to eat my lunch and then read various types of books. I read books on personal development, writing patents, constructing business plans, understanding finance, copyrights, trademarks, and other numerous topics. My reading never seemed to end, as the more I read, the more I realized how much I did not know.

My reading taught me that learning was something that would continue the rest of my life. The one thing over which I did have control was with what I would fill my brain. Would I fill my brain with much of the nonsense that exists in the world, or would I choose to fill it with information that would prove vital to my own success? I believe that I have chosen the latter of the two.

It is said that one of the most common attributes CEO's share is that they are well read. Being well-read is a choice, and it is something that is up to each individual. Being well-read shows not only intelligence, but also that the individual cares about the development of his or her brain.

The brain is the command post of our bodies. It can tell us to be lazy and not finish up on our necessary readings, or it can pitch the idea of reaching for the highest goals. Reading is a solitary act, and, oftentimes, one of the requirements to success is that the individual must first learn to do something solitary. This shows toughness and mental discipline. The more I read, the tougher I felt I was becoming in my mental preparation. I was, ultimately, preparing myself to begin to take small steps towards achieving the dreams and goals in which I believed so deeply.

The personal development seminar that I had attended after my graduate studies had ingrained within me the idea of reading in order to further personal development. With that said, my collection of books soon grew impressively, and I would often refer back to my notes on each book. With each book I read, I felt as if I were growing more intelligent. My thirst for knowledge would not be quenched, and I soon found myself reading constantly. Sometimes I would read a book three times over, such as was the case with understanding the different legal structures companies can take.

While on my quest to become better read and well-informed about financial topics in which I lacked knowledge, an amazing thing happened. After every book I completed reading, I noticed that each book contained about five to seven key words that were worthy of a whole book in themselves. Each time I finished a book, I had potentially around five more books that came from key words that existed in the book I had just completed. This is the amazing quality about reading; the more you read, the more you realize not only how much you do not know but also how much more reading you have left to do.

For time purposes, I was obviously not able to read all of the books that were derived from these key words. I tried to pick the topics that would most help me down the line. If one is looking to improve one's path down the road, I recommend reading topics with which you would like to be involved in the future. The key is to be as well-read in your field of expertise as possible. One obviously cannot know everything in a specific area or interest, but one certainly can know quite a bit.

Reading can be time-consuming and often falls victim to the same excuse as staying physically fit, that is a lack of or no time. As we all know, things that are time-consuming often get put aside. We say that we are waiting for a period when we have more time. The answer to this is that there will never be a good time, as there will always be something in our way. You must utilize your spare time for reading. Force yourself to read everything in which you are interested during your spare time.

Reading is one of the greatest investments in life that we can make. The key to knowledge and learning is to put reading at the top of your priority list. If television is that for which you have a true passion, then you should read as much as you can on the subject. You should treat it as your own personal assignment to read. I have taken it upon myself to learn all that I can. No one will help you learn or magically explain everything to you.

Keeping a reading list can help you along with the process. After college my aspirations and dreams for myself became substantially bigger than ever before in my lifetime. As a result of this, my reading list also grew to enormous proportions. I found myself reading everything that represented what I wanted to do in life. My reading list was always growing and continues to grow to this day. I asked colleagues and industry professionals for suggested reading materials that might help further my development. Each book can be seen as a piece of the puzzle that you are, ultimately, trying to complete in life.

Being well-read does more than just make you intelligent. It shows that you are an individual who has the will and patience to learn all that you can. I have always felt that my college degrees do not make me smarter than everyone else, but they do represent something. They represent a person with the discipline and determination to spend several years earning them. The same can also be said for reading books. Reading books signifies persistence and determination.

It is ironic that after earning my college degrees, I found myself learning far more than I ever did while in school. This can be true for anyone. No one should tell you that you cannot achieve something. Reading and knowledge are the keys to both freedom and intelligence. Once you unlock the door of learning, you may find that you turn something on inside of you which you never knew existed. I discovered that I had the spirit of an entrepreneur inside me. Through reading I learned that I had the desire and will to create.

Many entrepreneurs are motivated by creating something from nothing. It is the creative process that many are after, as well as the financial success that can come from entrepreneurial activities. They enjoy the challenge, and through reading I soon learned that these same beliefs were inside me. Reading allowed me to open a door to a world that I never knew was present inside of me, and you may find that it may do the same for you.

~

TIME MANAGEMENT

Once I entered the working world, I began to notice that most of my fellow employees liked to participate in office chatter. The problem that it presented was that of time management. I would work a solid eight hour day, achieving a good amount in a short amount of time, whereas other individuals would have to work eleven to twelve hour days as a result of their talking throughout the day. This chatter often consisted of negative gossip about other employees, useless information, and waste of time material in general.

I am not advocating for anyone to be anti-social. I am merely stating that most of the time one is better off just going about one's own business. I have heard, on numerous occasions, individuals make a bad comment about another employee to someone who they thought was trustworthy, only to find out that the so-called trustworthy individual had most likely leaked the information. A good rule of thumb with which to operate is the idea that negative comments will usually circulate to whomever they were intended. Therefore, it is best to mind one's own business and not participate in office chatter.

Many individuals love to gossip. It is what they do. I do not mean to belittle or put down these individuals. I am simply stating that gossip is not my style. In order to achieve a mentally fit brain, I took it upon myself to eliminate nonsense conversation. Individuals who participate in this do so because they have nothing else going on and are merely trying to entertain themselves. I was always entertained and had plenty of my own personal work in which to be engaged. Again, there is nothing wrong at all with talking to friends and colleagues while at work. However, when I heard some of the conversations in which my colleagues, friends, and random individuals participated, I realized that gossip and nonsense chatter were completely a waste of company's time and my time.

Having come from a sports and entertainment background, I always enjoyed discussing sports as I truly have a passion for them. An example that I still do not understand is the one of fantasy sports and betting on sports at work. Many of my colleagues throughout my entire working career participated in fantasy sports. When I was first exposed to this type of environment, I had nothing against them. I realized how consuming the fantasy sports were for certain individuals. I saw so many people wasting huge amounts of time and money on both fantasy sports and gambling; even the boss participated in such nonsense.

These two activities are not only time-consuming, but they hurt businesses and individuals themselves. It is estimated that companies lose massive amounts of money during the NCAA men's college basketball tournament each year in March. This is due to the fact that so many are worried about participating in office tournament brackets, and each day during March they are obsessed with following their bracket progress. Once again I think that March Madness is one of the best times of the year. I would advocate that people watch sports for the love of them but avoid activities that take away from personal time and business productivity.

Another topic that seems to reverberate across the office space setting of America is that of drinking. Ever since I have been a part of the working world, I often heard individuals talking about how intoxicated they were over the weekend. Is it possible for anyone else out there to think of a more useful and productive conversation topic? This type of discussion seemed to continue at every new place of employment in which I found myself early on out of college. These discussions would also leave me shaking my head, as I listened to individuals recount their crazy weekends. Once again this type of discussion seems fun and innocent to the casual observer, but upon closer examination it hints at exactly what is circulating and taking place in the minds of these individuals. What is taking place in their minds is often absolutely nothing.

Useless conversations will, ultimately, lead to one result, nothing. They will hinder one's time and lead to a bad use of time management. Nothing good will come from participating in them, and I encourage you to steer clear of them. Every time that I would find myself either listening or participating in one of these conversations, I felt as if I were a little less intelligent than before. I could literally feel my brain cells melting away. Do not demean yourself or others. Have respect for the opposite sex, do not participate in drunken conversations, and simply mind your own business when it comes to rumors. By also not participating in these conversations, you will be putting yourself a step ahead of these individuals mentally, socially, and professionally.

~

Oftentimes in business, companies will form a Limited Liability Company, more commonly referred to as an LLC. This is for the sole purpose of limiting the liability of its owners. The LLC revolves around the fact that a separate bank account is created for the company. This separates business funds from someone's own personal funds. In some circumstances a company can lose its LLC legal form by the commingling of personal and business funds.

Business can teach us a great deal about life, and, too often, it seems to be the case that many people fail to recognize how something completely random can directly correlate to themselves. The concept of a Limited Liability Company is not necessarily the first idea that would pop into someone's head with regards to what can help them in life. Neither would the idea of a sole proprietorship. However, these two legal forms are ideas that most people should be able to directly relate to their lives for further benefit and gains. If used properly, both of these legal forms should lead to a better, healthier, and more successful life for all willing to put forth the ideas discussed.

What one can take away from the LLC form is the idea of creating two separate bank accounts, not real bank accounts, but mental and emotional bank accounts. Too often it seems to be the case that people have no separation between their work life and their personal life, which can be another component of time management. One just seems to mold and cross right into the other. In a sense they are operating their lives like a sole proprietorship, where there is no separation between business and personal funds. Consequently, this can be one of the riskiest legal structures to enact, and the same can be said for living one's life in this manner.

Many people in life do not have a solid separation between their work and personal life. With the advent of new technology, it seems that many are now on call and answering emails twenty-four hours a day on their BlackBerry. For mental purposes there must be a break and separation between one's work and one's personal life. Otherwise, the two simply blend into one long day, week, month and eventually year.

Immediately after college graduation, I realized that in order to achieve the goals I set forth, I would have to create an

LLC around myself, having a separate mental bank account for work and a separate mental bank account for personal life. I operate on the principle that what happens at work stays at work. Work may never go exactly how we want or expect it to proceed. What is most important is to have a solid separation in life. What happens at home must stay at home as well.

One of the most important lessons I have learned so far is that in order to truly succeed in life, you will need to be both mentally sharp and mentally fresh. These are two tactics which must be firmly in place. I have seen so many of my colleagues become scatter-brained simply because they never set up two mental bank accounts. The simple notion that if work is not going well, all is not lost in the world is a very true belief. It is indeed possible to be finding success in one's personal life and projects and not be exactly where you want to be career-wise. Too often I have seen people let their work career affect their mental outlook and attitude on life. That simply is the wrong way to go about it.

Many of my close colleagues have reflected a negative and defeated attitude in the way that they go about living because work may not be going exactly as they planned. It is important to realize that if you work for someone else, you are theoretically on someone else's time when you are at work; therefore, you cannot always control the situation. Many of us in life like to have everything in order and be in complete control while we are at work, but the simple fact is that maybe we are working a job that will never fully be under control. Certain jobs always seem to have delays and backups with regards to paperwork. The question that needs to be addressed here is how individuals in this situation cope. They cope by setting up two separate mental bank accounts.

I have always prided myself on the fact that I feel that I operate my life truly under the principles of an LLC. The projects that I had going on while I was working were treated as completely separate, therefore ensuring as fresh a mental outlook as I could possibly maintain. It is important and vital to understand how many people in life operate their life like a sole proprietorship. They pile one thing on top of another until their life is a jumbled mess. Success is difficult when you do not separate entities, and it can lead to both stress and frustration.

One of the reasons many businesses operate under a sole proprietorship structure is because it is very easy and convenient to set up. This is probably why many people in life operate their life under the same principles as well, with no separation whatsoever. Take the time to ensure that you have good separation in your life. I promise it will be worth it in the end. Life is very much hustle and bustle these days, and any chance that we are able to put things into perspective will be an added bonus in our favor.

There is an old philosophy that states that when you are sweeping, you should be doing just that, simply sweeping. Many of us mentally relive our workday even when we are at home. This results in added tension, increased stress, and maybe even an unhealthy family life. Once work is over, it should be over. Leave it at the door. Set those parameters with your boss. There are always certain examples that allow for this philosophy to be untrue, but, for the most part, it is very true.

The idea of the sweeping philosophy can also be applied to work as well. Many individuals at work are unproductive simply because their minds are elsewhere. Perhaps they are thinking about family problems, the idea of finding a new job, or possibly none of the above. The point that is being made here is not only the idea of personal and professional separation, but also the idea of the soul being engrossed in what is being done at that exact moment. If one is relaxing, then that individual needs to be engrossed in relaxing instead of focusing on what needs to get done once the relaxing is over. This type of attitude will make one more effective and efficient while at work or whatever one may find oneself doing.

5

Financial Literacy

Financial literacy had never been a phrase that directly resonated with me. It was a phrase that was completely and utterly out of my vocabulary. Despite the fact that I was not aware of it, I was not alone. Many individuals are not aware of the term financial literacy. Directly stemming from this is the problem facing a wide range of people in today's challenging and competitive economy, not having a financial understanding of their money, how to make money, and how to spend money wisely.

What does it mean to be financially literate? According to my own thoughts and beliefs, it is individuals who have complete control over their finances. They are their own Chief Financial Officer. They know how to spend within their means, save for the future, and acquire assets which will make money for the duration of their lives as well as their children's lives. Investing in one's own financial literacy will be the best investment one ever makes.

The lack of financially literate people is a result of a lack of teaching certain habits and skills while in school. The school system is designed to produce individuals who will work for a living. This is known as earned income. Earned income is viewed as the way to make money. This is the old school of thinking, such as get a good job, save your money, invest your money wisely, and put it in the bank. This is the traditional education that most individuals receive in the area of financial literacy.

I quickly realized that I could not learn enough with regards to my own financial literacy. Certainly the old school of thinking would not be the only way to financial success. I had many years of missed learning to make up. It was not that what I had been taught in my youth was at all bad; it was just that I had a great deal of ground to cover. My acquired knowledge would soon begin to surpass my years of forced learning. I felt as if the more time I spent gaining knowledge of my own financial literacy, the stronger in the future I would become.

The great thing about education and learning is the more you learn, the more you realize how much you do not know. When I officially completed work on my Master's Degree, many friends and family greeted me with the usual, "I bet you're glad you won't have to do any more studying." This comprises most of the competition that we face in the world, individuals who only learn because they are forced to do so. I realized that my studying and learning had just begun. Any successful individual will tell you that learning is a lifelong process, it never ends, and it is best to know a little about a lot rather than a lot about a little. Learn all you can, and, most importantly, learn all you can about your own financial literacy and how to improve it significantly.

My own realizations regarding my quest for knowledge happened directly after the completion of my Master's Degree. Roughly two weeks after graduating, I departed for Australia with my family. It was there on the long train rides between cities that I realized I had not even begun to learn how to make it in the real world. During those train rides, I began to formulate different business ideas in my head and began to sketch the outlines of business plans on paper. My own personal goal, while in graduate school, was always to be a Division I Director of Athletics. It dawned on me while in Australia that I could never write up a single business plan or lead a Division I Athletic Department if I did not first build my financial literacy. It became very apparent that I was financially illiterate. I came to the harsh realization that I would need to improve my financial literacy or watch my dreams and aspirations fall by the wayside.

I instantly began to fight fire with fire. I began reading every financial book upon which I could get my hands on. Anything that would help improve my understanding of business, I considered worthy of my attention. I read books on how to build and construct business plans. In each book I paid particularly close attention to the financial section. The more numbers there were, the better. It was in these business plan books that I saw a world of knowledge to which I needed to pay close attention. My future depended on the way that I gripped and understood the world of business and its financial impact. I even began to watch many of the various financial channels that exist. As a child these were the channels that I quickly surfed through to get to sports. Now, these financial programs get a large part of my attention, and they should get a large part of your attention as well.

~

The trend for many middle class Americans is to buy and buy more once they receive a pay raise, financial bonus or even their regular paycheck. If one looks at the trend here, one would realize that this is not the wise thing to do. If someone receives a pay increase and that individuals spending habits increase exponentially as well, that person indeed has not earned a pay raise at all. The key to financial freedom is to have your money working for you, and, unfortunately, so many people in today's world do not understand this concept at all.

I realized that while I was working and saving my earned income, I also needed to have my earned income start working for me. The idea here would be for an individual such as myself to start acquiring assets. I would then use my assets to eventually purchase my liabilities. Most middle class Americans purchase their liabilities such as cars and boats with their earned income instead of with their assets. It really is not about being rich, poor, or middle class. It is all about being smart with how you use and make your money work for you. You can have $1 million and still be broke. On the other side of this scenario, you can have $50,000 and be more financially secure than the millionaire who is financially illiterate. Again, it is all about being smart with how you use and make your money work for you.

I began to examine the trends that are the plight of so many people. These trends would be occurring right in front of my very own eyes. I would see many of my professional colleagues come into money, and then instantly the next day they would show up with fancy liabilities. One of my colleagues had spent around $20,000 for a glamorous watch after receiving an inheritance. A smart individual would have taken the $20,000 that he came into and purchased an asset. That individual would then have waited for the asset to turn a positive cash flow and then go out to buy the watch. The idea of paying for liabilities with assets is a principle that is of extreme importance.

The other significant trend is that most individuals will look at a pay raise as a way to go out and purchase more goods. In economic terms, they would purchase "wants" and not "needs." A television would be considered a "want." Paying the electricity bill would be considered purchasing a "need." I use this example because I watched my colleagues earn their annual pay raise and on the very same day, even before the money became available in their bank accounts, purchase fancy televisions and stereos. One colleague had his power turned off for two months after his pay raise, but at least he had a nice new high definition television. I am not quite sure how he enjoyed that television since he had no electricity.

While purchasing "wants" is great for the economy, it is not good for the individual who earned the pay raise. Not only does that person not have a good understanding of financial literacy, but he or she is also impulsively giving in to personal desires quickly. It is this lack of financial literacy that, ultimately, prohibits many Americans from ever getting anywhere financially.

~

FINANCIAL LITERACY

Financial literacy is not addressed enough in society. We now live in a world where credit card debt is acceptable, and people do not know how to spend within their means. It is extremely easy to spend out of your budget when you physically do not see the transfer of money. The majority of people who go on spending sprees do so with the use of credit cards. For these unlucky individuals, the word financial literacy is simply not a part of their vocabulary. There is nothing literate about them when it comes to finances. Sadly enough, millions of individuals fall into this category. They have no concept of money, how to spend it, save it, or have their money work for them. Yes, credit is vital to our economy's success, but those who spend what they do not have will lose in the end.

Put this book down for a moment and count how many people you know who have credit card debt. I am pretty sure that you need more than one hand to count how many people you know who may be in this predicament. You might even need your feet to finish this counting. Americans spending money that they do not have is a cultural norm in today's society.

One week after turning eighteen, I received my first credit card in the mail with a $500 credit limit. One day later, my balance due was $500. For many young Americans that $500 eventually doubles, triples and quadruples until their credit spending is out of control. Okay, you get the picture and, hopefully, these quick spenders have learned their lesson. The fact is that you can still be financially literate. Stop spending. Only purchase your "needs." Do not invest until your credit cards are paid in full. I say this because where else can you earn a 15% to 30% return? Once your credit cards are paid in full, you are no longer paying interest. If my colleague who paid $20,000 for the fancy watch had a credit card balance of $10,000 over a one year period, this would be about $2,000 in interest. Someone financially literate would have taken that $20,000 and paid off the $10,000 credit card balance and invested the other $10,000.

In America new areas of concern are always growing and developing. Our schooling systems do not prepare individuals for the financial challenges that they will all face throughout their lives. There are no classes that teach children at an early age how to spend and save responsibly. Classes such as these would serve great purpose by educating individuals and preparing them for a very financially motivated lifestyle.

This appears to be a growing trend in America and one that continues to plague many people throughout their adult lives. Financial literacy is an issue which should be addressed at any stage of an individual's life. There simply is not too young of an age to improve financial prowess. Many friends began their understanding of basic financials by playing children's board games like Monopoly. However, the sign of today's times are very apparent through today's versions of Monopoly. I find it troubling that today's Monopoly boards incorporate credit cards and other lines of credit. What happened to buying Boardwalk or Park Place with money saved in the bank?

~

Having this new understanding of financial literacy, I began to explain all that I had been learning to my close colleagues. They would be the ones to inform me whether I made sense or no sense at all. I painted the picture of where my financial literacy quest had taken me and how it could help them out in their own lives. My sessions soon began to last several hours with my colleagues as I strived to educate them on everything I had been learning over the course of my readings. I started with basics and then moved on to more advanced topics.

Once I got to the more advanced topics, I began to have followers who were truly listening to the message at hand. This message was one about changing the traditional view of money and how it worked. An amazing thing happened while I was teaching my colleagues; I began to find myself understanding the topics even better and becoming better in regards to my own financial literacy.

It is said that if you really want to learn something in life, you must first learn it yourself, and then teach it to others. By teaching it to others, you will be putting your comprehension of the topic to the test. It is easy to grasp and understand a topic on your own, but the real test comes when you must explain it to another. My knowledge of financial literacy was growing during these lecture sessions that I would have with friends.

~

While hard at work on improving my financial literacy, I also learned that it was hard to make a dollar while working for others. The more money I would make, the more I would, unfortunately, pay in taxes. I realized that while I would not quit my day job, I would begin to take the steps necessary to slowly free myself from the chains that connected me to my earned-income lifestyle. Do not quit your day job, but always be on the look-out for something that can positively improve your financial literacy. This might include paying off your debt, looking for that dream job which will help increase your earned income, making smart investments, and purchasing real estate.

I began to gather with friends to contemplate investing in property or ideas. While the goal of this book is not to discuss investment strategy or projects, this book is also important for all those wishing to escape the so-called normal lifestyle. I educated myself on the best areas in which to acquire property and projects. Such projects included rental properties, on-line businesses, consulting agencies, communications, and much more.

All can be lucrative endeavors, but you must be financially literate to have any chance of success.

While contemplating on various investments, I realized an important lesson that making money was a goal. However, it was not my sole driving factor. I found this statement hard to believe, given the fact that many of the ideas I had circulating in my head called for millions of dollars in order to be effectively launched. What got me out of bed aggressively each morning was the fact that I wanted nothing more than to see my ideas fly. It was never about the money because I knew that I was more financially literate than I was in the past. I would spend such a great amount of time nurturing my mind and building my financial literacy that I felt as if I were ready to see my ideas take wings and take that first calculated risk out into the open air. This was a defining moment for me because it represented what I had been searching for all along.

The key to doing something great is to find things that are your passion, meaning you cannot wait to go to bed and get up in the morning. This is exactly what I valued. This is living life. It was the belief that I felt as if I owed it to myself to see my dreams through, no matter how unrealistic they may have appeared. We only have one life, and if you have a great passion for something, do not be afraid to take that first calculated jump off of the tree and away from the nest. However, being financially literate provides a solid foundation in achieving such desired goals.

6

The Networking Lottery

It has been said that it is not what you know, but it is who you know. My view on networking would indicate that I am an advocate for the power of meeting individuals and networking, but I would warn against relying on this for future gains and growth. This is a very dangerous route in my opinion. To put one's future in the hands of another is about one of the most dangerous things of which I can possibly think. Despite this, I still feel as if networking can be extremely beneficial to all individuals. Let's face it! To get that good job you probably will need to know someone, but at the same time you cannot count on that person to get you a job. It is fair to say that I am a strong believer in making your own opportunities and playing what I like to refer to as the networking lottery.

Networking is something that I have been doing since before my undergraduate work and still do so to this day. Every week I try to establish contact with people pertinent to my field. In today's changing technological times, it is now easier to contact individuals, yet despite this people often do not respond due to the heavy flux of emails that they may receive. Despite the fact that I continue to network, I remain heavily skeptical of the whole process. I continue to play the game but, ultimately, take the attitude that nothing will happen as a result. It ensures that I constantly try to create my own opportunities instead of counting on others to help me out.

The networking lottery is something in which many people participate, but I think very few people actually play right. It seems that most think networking is all about going to a social function and exchanging business cards. This is one of the many steps in the lengthy process. The first step in the networking lottery phase is to exchange business cards, followed by an email or phone call, potential meeting, and lastly, a continuance to keep in touch.

Networking is more than just handing someone your business card. Once you have done so, you have then been invited to build a relationship on a personal level with that person. This relationship-building process can take anywhere from one day to one year, depending on how busy the individual might be.

THE NETWORKING LOTTERY

I always operate on the principle that sometimes it could take three to four months of continuous contact before someone would take me seriously. Once the point would come when I was taken seriously, I am then usually invited to a meeting with that individual or group. After the initial meeting, even if nothing came from it, I would still view it as having one more contact in the industry. The more contacts you have, the better off you will be. Networking is a long and lengthy process, and it is a great deal like building a strong relationship, in that it takes time, nurturing, and care.

~

During my initial time after earning my graduate degree, I began to see exactly what was wrong with networking. Most young individuals believe that networking involves simply going to an outing, shaking someone's hand, and handing off a business card. Shockingly, I have seen many who do not even follow up with the contacts they meet. It is as if they believe that just because they handed their card to someone, that person is automatically going to contact them at a later time and date.

In all of my networking experiences, I do not ever remember someone contacting me. I always had to go looking for that person. Most networking does not work simply because both parties are merely passing out business cards.

YOU HAVE A COLLEGE DEGREE, NOW WHAT?

One lesson I learned from my days in sales was that you need to sell a business opportunity to someone and not just merchandise. Most sales people are selling a product. The true business man knows, for the most part, that this type of approach does not work. I learned that nothing sparks someone's interest more than a business plan or business proposal. I have seen that if someone smells a good business opportunity, he or she will come looking for you. This has happened a few times to me when I merely submitted my executive summary from one of my many business plans to a key business contact. I recall a certain instance where I submitted my executive summary to a gentleman who had successfully created two large and highly competitive companies. He, in fact, contacted me three times. He recognized a potential business opportunity.

The key is to sell a business opportunity and not merely be looking for a job or handout. Individuals have nothing to gain from helping someone who is merely looking for something for free. If you suddenly start to present yourself as a person who has a potential business opportunity for someone, you will soon find that people will come looking for you.

It is fair to say that most successful people have also been the most persistent. Yes, there is that word again, and it holds true with the networking lottery. If you are trying to get into contact with people in your field, send them an email about every two weeks for approximately three to four months. At times you may feel like you are bothering these people. Often quite the opposite has occurred. It has been my experience that these people will usually meet me and will be impressed that I have taken the time over the course of three to four months to contact them. They are impressed by the persistence.

It can be frustrating to individuals who are new to the networking game because it usually takes many emails and phone calls before an individual will take another individual seriously. I have learned this firsthand. Many prominent people in organizations have said to me, "The only reason why I am meeting with you is because you have quietly pursued me over the past three to four months." I have had two job interviews that have taken four months, from the time I first began the communication process to when I actually sat down and interviewed for a position. Success takes time, and those who learn this concept will be able to achieve many things that most will not.

Other helpful hints for playing the networking lottery are simple tactics that everyone should execute. After your meeting you should prepare a personalized thank you note to that individual thanking him or her for their time. Do not forget the secretary, too. You would be surprised how many times the contact will ask the secretary his or her thoughts, so send them a note, too. Always ask the people with whom you meet if they know of anyone who may be able to help. Send holiday cards to all of your contacts who are in your networking database. Check in with them throughout the year, especially if you have a business opportunity to share with them. Do not be afraid to network with people outside of your industry because you never know where that may lead. You never know who they might know in your current industry. Above all else, just be yourself!

~

I encourage all to play the networking lottery because if you do not play, you simply cannot win. With that said, people should still be striving to make their own opportunities. Put your faith directly into the wind and bore full steam ahead. The idea that others can and will help you is a risky endeavor indeed, but there are individuals who truly do care. These individuals are the ones who remember what it was like to try and break into an industry. It is important to remember that everyone had to start somewhere. Even the founders of the largest companies in the world were once essentially nobodies. The next time you walk into the President's office of a large corporation, realize that he or she, too, was once unknown. Everyone has to start somewhere.

7

Leadership

There are many responsibilities a college graduate has in the workforce such as executing personal brand, time management, demonstrating financial literacy, playing the networking game, and maintaining persistence. However, the biggest responsibility of all is being a great leader. There are a number of entry-level managers, mid-level managers and senior-executives in today's business world who are in leadership roles but do not have a clue of what good leadership consists of. With many organizations recruiting college graduates for leadership roles, the emphasis on being a leader could not be greater. After earning my college degrees and gaining experience in the workforce, I believe there are six essential components of knowing how to become a successful leader and how to keep that leadership role where one can succeed as a true, genuine leader.

~

Leading by example consists of being a role model for others who look to you for guidance. This means that as a leader, you cannot go hang out at your local bar because your employees may see you. You must lead by example to earn your employees' respect and trust. A company watches senior management; the employees look to leaders as role models, and each leader must work very hard living up to that. Being a professional leader and leading by example requires thinking about it everyday. It is essential to study leadership, read, go to classes, and even watch movies of good leadership based on great persons such as Gandhi, Martin Luther King, Nelson Mandela, and so many more. Everyday leaders have to learn about the world, but more importantly they must learn about themselves.

Leading by example also means showing a combination of enthusiasm and loyalty to the company, and it certainly means demanding excellence in the organization. Leaders need to constantly demonstrate what it is for which they care so greatly. It is important to be authentic; do not be a big shot and pay attention to all people. Know that as an executive or any level of leader, those in charge are there to serve others and not be served. A leader should never raise his or her voice or make people do things. A good leader should convince others to do what needs to be done even if it takes a little longer. If a leader can demonstrate these qualities, the team will have 100% trust because they know the leader is trustworthy.

Leaders often forget about the fundamentals of their job, but successful leaders never forget how they got there and where they need to go. One problem leaders run into is the ability to manage their time. The reason many leaders do not manage their time is because they are not organized enough. This is one of the worst ways to lead by example in an organization.

When in doubt, do what your mother would. Each great leader for whom I have worked always agreed that the best way to be an example to the organization is to act as your mother would have acted when it came to managing time. One of my greatest leaders reminded me to always leave time in my calendar to meet with whomever calls because my mother would have done so. Being a parent is the most important leadership position in the universe, so I recommend that if you manage like your mother, you will lead by example.

~

Leading a company also means being there for people. In doing so, a leader must focus on the people upon whom they have an impact daily and should be available to them. As a leader sometimes you just have to be there with your people.

You have to be in the same room with them, look them in the eyes, and hear their voices. You might hold a management position, but leadership is about influence and doing the right things for the people in the organization. If you have an organization that is small enough, being there simply means having contact with employees, and making yourself available to them. When the organization gets bigger, it is unbelievably frustrating to a good leader that he or she cannot be there for everyone.

Being there for people also means having a heart, especially when difficult decisions involve people, as they normally do. I personally believe that the best route to the brain is through the heart. A leader has to get into people's hearts first to make them believe the company is doing the right things and doing so in a way where they feel appreciated. At the beginning of most leaders' careers, for example, they do not fully appreciate their responsibilities as a leader. The main responsibility of being there for people is having a good heart and being open to the needs of the organization's workforce.

Making decisions is part of every leader's job description, no matter how difficult the decision may be. Most of my executive peers wince when it comes to making difficult decisions, but all of their approaches are similar and very effective. Tough decisions can be managed in such a way that employees feel good about them, not angry, unappreciated, or even misunderstood. Making decisions in an organization falls under being there for people because when you make a decision, it involves people and possibly their lives, whether it is good or bad.

~

A leader must be a nudge or a motivator. If a leader is motivated, the employees will follow with motivation. As a leader I sometimes have to nudge my employees by lighting a fire under them, but this is the last resort option. Leaders must constantly remind people of ideas and follow up because good ideas have a way of getting lost. Good ideas have a way of falling through the cracks, or they get mired in bureaucracy, and everyone is busy in their own universe. It is clear that sometimes all that good ideas or good people need is an advocate who will not shut up. Great leaders will bug their employees until they get it right because it is too good of an idea to waste. Motivate them that it is okay to take the risk.

~

Showing creative leadership is very important in today's business world because of tight budgets and different views of fiscal responsibility. A creative leader can take a little and make it into a lot. It is better if good ideas, rather than bad ideas, come from the top. However, ideas can come from anywhere. The leader in any type of business should be creative. A leader should be spouting ideas all the time, just like everyone else in the organization. Many leaders come up with ideas driving to work, walking around the house, watching kids at sporting events and everywhere else. It can become addictive.

Many ideas coming from the top, however, can also be bad. It is essential that employees inform their leader that an idea is bad. In return, the leader must accept the criticism with an open mind. When I was in my first leadership role out of college, many of my ideas were simply bad, and, believe me, I was told quickly. That kind of honesty in a team needs to exist, but only you can ensure that it does.

~

Leaders must communicate to their subordinates, but they must also take the time to listen. Listening is not only an essential fundamental in the communication process, but also in the leadership process as well. While working for an organization during college, a co-worker and I had an idea that could have helped fix a scheduling issue between another employee and me. The two of us approached our leader to explain our very direct and clear idea. After a few days it seemed as if we had never spoken to our leader, and the issue was never resolved.

I never could understand what happened until becoming a leader myself. I learned that some leaders can fake listening, but successful leaders will listen and listen carefully to their employees. What I learned was that our leader was not listening to our needs and, in a sense, was being dishonest with us. Leaders who listen with great detail will take the input and apply it to the appropriate areas of an organization. If a leader does not listen and fakes it, those decisions may affect others without them even knowing it. Such was the case with my co-worker and I at this prominent organization. As a future leader, I planned on never making the mistake of "not listening," and to this day I always listen to my employees. If I am too busy or cannot provide an employer or employee my undivided attention, I will be honest with them and arrange another time in my calendar. Sometimes it is best to just stop what I am doing to listen, which is the best route to ensure good employer/employee relationships.

~

The most important leadership strategy is undoubtedly integrity. Every great leader with whom I come into contact will agree that integrity and honesty are the most important qualities a leader must have. As a leader I focus on doing the right thing, being honest, ethical and respectful of all people. My employers know to never ask me to do anything dishonest or unethical. I talk about this with them before I go to work for them. A leader must know for what principles he or she stands as well as which will not be tolerated if they are unethical. An instant "no" should come right out of a leader's mouth if ever asked to do something unethical or dishonest. The newspaper is full of leaders who were not ready and are now going to jail. Integrity must begin at the start of one's career and not at the latter part of it. When in doubt, do the right thing, always.

Integrity may involve ethics and doing the right thing, but some of the toughest problems leaders face are the loss of a job. As a leader if one has both integrity and ethics when dealing with the loss of an employee's job, the entire situation will be better on both sides. It is, therefore, important to be honest with employees and let them know where they stand. After a termination occurs, real leaders will continue to help until the employee lands back on his or her feet. Helping an employee recuperate from job loss involves a great deal of integrity, just like everything else associated with being a leader.

I have had to terminate a few employees in my career due to company directives, and these were difficult decisions. Nonetheless, I helped each of the terminated employees recover from this situation in any way I could. I assisted them with the unemployment paperwork, provided them with letters of recommendations, referrals to fellow contacts, and any other career direction I could provide.

~

Learning to be an effective leader involves more than reading a textbook. These six leadership strategies are so essential to succeeding as a leader because they are focused and direct. In addition, the strategies and lessons come from real life experience. However, becoming a successful leader does not occur overnight. It is important to not worry about climbing the corporate ladder, but concentrate on learning as much information as possible. In doing so, the corporate and leadership jobs will fall into place like a perfectly made spider web. Working with some of the most powerful leaders in today's business world, the realization is that becoming a great leader is a process, which is what most leaders fail to acknowledge. During the process of becoming a great leader, it is important to remember that many days will be tougher than the one before. As a leader, this idea must be accepted; if not, failure is imminent. Finally, as a leader you cannot have the enormous highs without the deep lows.

8

Take Control of Your Life

I am a firm believer in the idea that only you can help yourself. Oftentimes it seems like individuals get lucky and fall into a great job, but these circumstances are the exception and not the norm. I encourage everyone to feel empowered as if you and only you can, ultimately, determine the outcome of your life. I am not advocating that everyone stop working and networking. I am simply stating that it is up to each individual to determine how far he or she will go in life. Once I came to the realization that I controlled my own destiny, I was free to go about life not worrying about circumstances. A colleague of mine once stated, "I'm sitting around waiting for less educated people than myself to determine my future." This is a true statement for many individuals in today's workforce. There are a great number of extremely intelligent individuals out there who are waiting for others to determine their future. I took on the mindset early in life that I would determine exactly what I was capable of accomplishing.

We all have special talents that may be hidden. They remain hidden because we live in a world where ideas are often crushed by individuals who are negative and who did not have the gumption and persistence to pursue their own ideas. Achieving success is about freeing the human mind of rational thought and allowing it to expand to dimensions that might be seen as not being part of reality. To come up with a big idea, one must be free of rational reasoning and explore the boundaries that exist beyond reality.

Some of the greatest ideas of our time have come when individuals abandoned reality. This type of free thinking can lead to great outcomes, and I encourage all to have brainstorming sessions where one thinks beyond regular constraints. Oftentimes companies or corporations like individuals who fit into the cookie cutter mold of not thinking outside of the box, or puppets as I like to call them, but the truth is that real leaders and great inventors lead rather than follow. Lead in your own way and avoid being a follower at all costs.

The older I have become, the more I have realized that only you can help yourself. No one is going to do it for you. I cannot tell you how many times people have said that they wanted to help me. Many times these were teachers who I once had.

It is funny that, in a sense, if you put a group of individuals in a room, provide alcoholic beverages with food, and call it a social mixer, all of a sudden everyone wants to help. My own belief is that once the alcohol is flowing freely, the amount of lies and amount of people who want to help you increase exponentially. People want to build themselves up to be bigger than they really are. "I would like to help you, and I will introduce you to my friend who is the head of this large company." These words still sicken me to this day.

Often in my young and naive years, I would fall for these traps and begin to contact these individuals once I had returned home. I realized that they would then disappear into the mist and fog of lies and false promises from whence they came, never to be heard from again. Why is this true? People like to build themselves up. I have always been of the opinion that if you have to tell someone how big and great you are, then you are not that big after all. You are a small-time person. Small-time people have to build themselves up. Great people are armed with an inner confidence that almost seems to seep out of their pores. Be an individual who is an egoless person portraying self-confidence from within.

TAKE CONTROL OF YOUR LIFE

~

This is a great time to begin calling out certain individuals who I have known throughout my career who are not only full of themselves, but simply full of it. They seem to be infesting the corporate world at an alarming rate. They will offer you no help whatsoever. They simply like to toot their own horn and show everyone how great they think they are. These certain individuals have served as great motivation throughout the course of my career. They are firsthand evidence of something that I have felt for quite some time now. I cannot emphasize enough that only you can help yourself. Once you come to the realization that each individual in life can only help himself or herself, you will be headed in the correct direction.

If you do find yourself encountering people who are constantly making false promises to you, I would take a very simple approach. With each false person with whom you speak, consider it as if you are adding more fuel to the fire. When it is all said and done, you will have a fire that is a blazing inferno. Use this fire as a wall of motivation, wanting to prove to yourself that you do not need help from anyone.

If you want to do something, not only will others often not help you, they often do not care either. Many people frequently do not care about anyone but themselves. You do not need others to be able to stand on your own two feet. When you stumble, as we all do from time to time, the only person who will be there to pick you up is you. Pick yourself up, and, ultimately, rise above all those who simply talk a big game.

Success in life, for the most part, is up to each individual. If you want to give up, no one is going to stop you. If you want to wait for others to help you, no one is going to help you. However, if you take your future into your own hands, you will be taking the first step towards ultimately be that guiding hand that we all need.

~

It is a very empowering feeling knowing that you will not stop, you will not rest, and you will, ultimately, succeed. Most highly successful people will tell you to just keep going. One of the most important lessons I learned after college revolved around motivation and work ethic. If you find yourself working as hard as you can and are not getting anywhere, simply keep going. It is the ones who jump off of the ride and quit who will not get to where they want to go.

It was also a comforting feeling knowing that if I worked as hard as I could and still did not accomplish what I set out to do, I would be able to look myself in the eye and feel proud knowing that I gave it every ounce of energy I had. This is a large part of being in control of your life. You may not be able to control the outcome of what you set out to do, but you can control the way you go about accomplishing things.

Throughout our lives we will undoubtedly have people telling us that we cannot do this or achieve that. These people should serve as motivation in our lifetime. Many have told me exactly the same. Some have said that they could not picture me achieving some of the goals that I have laid out. They served and still serve as serious motivation today. You also should be motivated as I was by those who doubted me.

Motivation is something which should not be underestimated for a second. It provides the ability to either keep going or quit. Those who keep going are, undoubtedly, motivated, and those who quit are simply not. It would be a lie to say that everyone is not motivated by finances to some degree. If we were not motivated by money, then we would not work. Many are motivated by money. I have determined that in my lifetime, I am most motivated by my ideas and dreams. I want to see my ideas take shape, be enacted, and, ultimately, take wings and fly off. I encourage you to not be motivated by money. It is important that you find from where your motivation comes and what motivates you on a daily basis.

How many people each year around New Years say that they are going to get in better shape? The more important question is how many of them follow through with their promise to themselves? Successful people do not feel motivated for one week; they are always motivated. My problem is not motivation at all; it is turning it down at the end of the night. It is key to remain motivated at all times. Motivation is healthy and forces you to step out of your comfort zone in order to reach for new heights. Reach for the highest goals you possibly can, and you may just achieve those goals.

Motivation is something which I hope I can possess all my life. Wielded correctly it can lead to great things. It has the possibility to make us all feel as if we can accomplish anything. Those who are unmotivated may have once wielded its power, yet for some reason or another it has escaped them. The flame inside that once burned has been extinguished permanently. I have seen from my own personal experiences from friends and colleagues that once motivation is lost, it is tough to regain. The key is to make sure that you never lose it. Treat it as importantly as you can because it may often help you when all other lights in your world have gone out. Motivation has caused me to read more, think deeper, and, ultimately, set out to accomplish what I know I can do. It has spurred business plans, brainstorming sessions, and many other ideas. The idea that I am possessed by motivation has been a topic of discussion by individuals close to me. I do not see it as a bad thing if used correctly. You do not want your life to become completely obsessed with success and business, but without motivation it is tough to get anywhere.

Motivation is at its highest when someone is trying to launch something or make it big. This is when motivation might be the only driving force. How do you keep going when all others around you might be telling you to call it quits? This is a common question. The answer is to look deep within yourself and see exactly what it is that motivates you. We will all be motivated by different factors. Whether we want to believe it or not, we all have parts of us that tell us we cannot do something. In this sense sometimes you also have to prove to yourself that you can accomplish a certain goal.

~

Life is not confusing, but it is people who make it confusing by not having a clear path that they set out for themselves. Having a desired set of goals in one's life is absolutely vital. Goals allow an individual to begin to see the course that they must take. I began to follow my own path, only interested in things that would help me. It is important to realize that there are many things and people in life that can hurt and hinder your progress down your own path. I only wanted to be surrounded by positive and motivated people like myself. I began to rid myself of everyone who did not meet this criteria, for they are parasites and did not positively motivate me in any way.

When dealing with goals and dreams, one must also address the issue of failing. If one looks at the portfolio of a very successful individual, one might be surprised to find a series of failures. Success often does not happen during the first, second, third, or even fourth attempt. Oftentimes it is the individual who sticks with it who will find success. This often results in a portfolio of failures. The smart and successful individual will learn from each and every failure, and the next time they will be just that much smarter. Learning from mistakes and failures is one of life's great lessons. The individuals who are able to learn the most from these mistakes are the ones who will prevail in the end.

Many individuals feel as if a failure is their chance to show the world how they will rebound and bounce back. Some people let their failures define them, while others choose to define their failures. If you choose the latter, you will never fear failure because you know that you will not let your failures define you. This is a very empowering mindset, and I adopted this philosophy early on in my career. Once you take on this belief, you will feel as if there is nothing you cannot do or overcome. You simply feel as if you can do it all.

It will make launching that next great venture that much easier. Life is too short to sit and dwell on failures of the past. If you have failed, get up, dust yourself off, reflect on what you did wrong, and what you will do differently next time around. Use your failure or failures as self motivation to achieve whatever it may be for which you are striving. Persevere and do not give up. There simply is no other way to overcome failure than to counteract it with dogged persistence and an iron will. If you stay at something long enough, you eventually will succeed.

I compare my own portfolio of failures to that of driving. When I am driving with someone and that person is showing me how to get somewhere, I will only feel that I know the road and correct way once I have driven the route on my own. The same can go for launching an idea or being successful. Many people have great ideas, but few follow through and actually enact them. The reason for this, I believe, is that people are looking for books or a road map on how to actually initiate various ideas. From my own experiences with speaking to various individuals who have launched business ventures, sometimes there is no road map on how to actually do something. You will only know how to do something once you do it. If you are going to put together a television channel, you simply need to do it, because for the most part there is not a book which will take you step-by-step. Get out in the trenches, make the mistakes, and just do it! Many of the ideas that I have been working on, and am still working on to this day, have no manuals on how to go about doing them. I have always operated on the principle that I would figure out the problems as they arose.

I also believe that by putting myself out there, I would be opening myself up to failure and criticism. Failure is as much a part of business as success is. If success exists, then it is only logical that failure exists, too. I would encourage everyone to reprogram their brains with regards to what exactly failure is and what it constitutes. Failure should not be called failure; it should aptly be called learning experiences. A failure is when one fails, falls down, and does nothing to get back up. A learning experience happens when one fails and resurrects to his or her feet with a vengeance. This is when failure is not failure at all, rather a positive lesson learned.

~

My own self-belief and internal fortitude came over the period of a half year. It took many hours each day of soul searching, but once I found it I realized I was forever changed. During the first summer after I completed graduate school, all those around me were coincidentally traveling around the globe, leaving me to myself. At first I felt extremely lonely, as if I did not have a friend in the world. It was during this time that I took a long walk on a nearby path in the wilderness. I was in a zone, walking, thinking, and witnessing nature. I thought about how hard things seemed and how it was almost impossible to make contact with certain people, let alone achieve success. I realized on that walk that I was fine with how hard the road looked because I felt as if I were taking the necessary steps. Things just felt right, every action everyday felt right.

I cannot stress how important self-belief is. Self-belief will always be there to pick you up when you are all alone. We are all on our own to some degree. When I completed my graduate degree, I realized that I was all on my own, and it was up to me to push myself over the edge. Nobody would magically be there to lend a hand or an extra boost of confidence. My parents and family did a superb job of raising me, but, unfortunately, after entering into the real world it became evident that they could not help me. They had done all they could to instill proper morals and beliefs into me, and now it was up to me to put them to good use.

This way of thinking emphasizes taking one's own life into one's own hands. We all need to pick ourselves up from time to time. If you do not pick yourself up, no one will be there to do it for you. Having a strong self-belief is one of the attributes that separates the truly successful individuals from the mediocre ones. Be your own best friend, and help yourself to success.

My will to succeed, for the most part, exceeds my fear of failing. I refuse to believe that I cannot do something. This is a belief and philosophy that I have held my entire life. Ever since I was a little child, I have always believed that anything and everything is possible. The sad thing about life is that as we grow older, we lose that youthful exuberance. Do not lose it because it is priceless.

As I progress further along in my life, encountering more and more negative people on a daily basis, I am constantly reminded that the only person I intend to follow in life is myself. When you take the approach that you are only going to follow yourself, you are basically admitting that you will be taking the path less traveled. This path can be intimidating because so many choose not to take it. Most are content to follow the actions of others. I have made up my mind that I am not content to follow others and will go to great lengths to make sure that I follow my own beliefs. We all have different beliefs, and that is what leads to the diversity that we see in everyday life. It all comes down to two simple questions. Will you follow yourself or follow the actions of others? Will you take the path less traveled, or will you take the path traveled by most?

Self-belief is something with which many struggle. It comes from deep within and represents parts of the subconscious that exist in us all. Do you have what it takes to make it? This is a question that I often ask myself. The answer is always yes.

I feel that the difference between someone who makes it big and someone who does not is a matter of inches.

One could definitely argue the different factors that could be present with this type of situation. I would often look at extremely successful people and ask what it was that they possessed that others did not? One of the key factors that most of these individuals possess is that of self-belief. They are armed with this particular feeling that is as strong as nails. It is this self-belief that helps them travel down the path that is less traveled. This is a point of separation that should be looked at with great clarity and insight. It is this strong belief in one's self that can literally propel individuals up from the masses.

Self-belief is one of the most powerful forces we possess, and I would encourage you to use it as your strength. It is to your credit to have a strong sense of self-belief matched with an iron will. Defeat is for the weak with no sense of it. With self-belief will undeniably come victory for all those who wield its immense power.

~

Reality can, at times, be our worst enemy because it tells us what we can and cannot do. I personally am not a fan of reality. It is the enemy of dreams and hopes. It holds individuals down, and, in some cases, paralyzes certain people into fear.

Reality is that little voice in the back of your head that says "You cannot do that, it's impossible." I believe that nothing is impossible, and if I ever stopped believing this then I would cease to exist. It is what motivates me, the belief that our lives are like a blank sheet of canvas. We are the painters, and we are the ones who decide what goes on the canvas and which direction the portrait takes. My goal is to have no room left on the canvas. I want to do everything I can in my lifetime. I would also include my failures on the canvas because I value them and see them as learning experiences. They represent who I am and have served as great motivators over the years.

Reality can often be extremely cruel because it tells us exactly how it is. I am a firm believer in letting your mind enter into other realms in order to come back to reality with a greater understanding of the power of thought. Our mind is the most powerful muscle that we possess, and we should use it to our greatest advantage. I have, from time-to-time, called upon my brain to help me out. Allow yourself to have brainstorming activities where you think up wild and crazy ideas. Many of your ideas will, most likely, be silly and humorous, but if you enact this strategy enough, you will probably find that you will eventually hit upon a solid idea. This type of thinking frees the mind from the constraints that society and the world have put on it. Most people fail to realize that we are all somewhat limited by our thought. For many people, society has told them what they can and cannot do. This is a sad, but very true, reality.

One idea that has always spurred me on is the thought of how bad it would be to go about life if I had already come to the preconceived notion of what I could achieve in life. For many in the world, this simply is their existence. Brainstorming activities help represent the beginning of freeing one's brain from the chains of mankind that constantly drag it down. If we let it, society will drag us down and down, until one day we go completely under. Fight back, and do not give in. Rise against the chains that constantly try to pull you down.

~

If you can dream it, then it would only make sense to believe that you can live and achieve it. Be a doer and a dreamer. In order to be a doer, you must first be a dreamer. Soon after completing my graduate degree, I realized that I had large goals and expectations of myself. It was my goal to try and achieve most or all of these. I learned that it is okay to aim for the top of Mount Everest. It is your life, and you should be able to aim wherever you please with regards to your goals and dreams. Do not ever let anyone tell you otherwise because there are many who, in a sense, could be called dream destroyers. They like to rain on the parade of others because it is most likely the case that someone once rained on their dreams. Do not let these negative individuals get in your way because they lurk in all parts of life. They come in all shapes and sizes.

One thing that remains clear about these dream destroyers is the message that they bring forth. They serve to crush all dreams and aspirations of others. Do not give in, do not let them win. Giving in to them is the easy way out. Use your mind and figure a way to make your dreams and goals a reality.

Our brains control every action we make and take. Make every action that you take worthwhile. Always remember that thought can lead us to great innovations, and it is through thought that great milestones and achievements are made. Do not limit your thought to the boundaries of reality. Allow it to expand and enter into the deep realms of the subconscious that is within us all. It is fair to say that most people have had their dreams stepped on and destroyed and, therefore, do not allow deep thought to take place within their brains. Do not be one of those persons because when your dreams cease to exist, you yourself cease to exist.

~

A business man once told me that if you do not have critics, then you are not doing your job. When I first heard this, I had to pause for a moment and think about what exactly that statement meant. If you do not want critics, then all you simply have to do is not put yourself out there on public display for all to see. By putting yourself within public view, you are not only increasing your overall odds for success, but you also are, ultimately, doing your job. This is an important lesson that I learned and instantly took to heart.

I look at putting yourself out there as the same way as playing the lottery. If you do not play the lottery, then you definitely have no chance of winning. By continually putting one's self on public display, the chances for success are greater. I am a firm believer that if individuals keep working at their goals and aspirations, then it is only a matter of time before they break through and succeed. Success comes to individuals who refuse to give up until they reach their dreams and aspirations. I consider it a sin to go through life with dreams in the back of one's head, to simply do nothing about them, and to just leave them there. If you have an idea in your head, do not at all be afraid to pursue it. Taking the first step to pursue one's ideas and dreams is the hardest part of the process. Getting the courage to enter unfamiliar territory can, at times, be a scary venture in itself, but you simply owe it to yourself to pursue your dreams.

Putting yourself out there can be intimidating. It can mean putting yourself into potential situations in which you might not be experienced. With that said, it is important that you take the initial step. It is very easy and tempting just to sit back and exist, never taking risks at all. Nothing is guaranteed, and there will always be risks. We can decrease risk by the more we know. Remember, knowledge is freedom, and the more we know, the less risk we will face in life.

~

Oftentimes successful people who have made it big in business are asked how they took that initial first step. The usual response seems to be to find something you love. It is important to have passion because it is passion that drives us in those early stages. When we are just starting out in a career or trying hard to launch a business, passion will play a huge part in whether we continue or give up. Nothing comes easy, and anything that is worthwhile will usually take time. It is the degree of difficulty and time issue that keep most from ever pursuing their true passions. Things take time, and they usually are extremely difficult. It is important to not be afraid of either. The bottom line is that it is hard to make it big in life, and it is most definitely hard to earn a dollar. Neither comes easy nor fast.

Since completing my graduate degree, it has been my goal to make myself known with my various projects and interests. Only then would I truly feel as if I were a part of the game. Failure to do so would make me feel as if I were like most, sitting back waiting for an opportunity. Do not do this because that opportunity may never come. Create your own opportunities by going out and making yourself known. It simply is a numbers game, meaning the more times you make others aware of you, the more chances you inevitably have for success. Above all else, take control of your life early on and keep control of it until you reach your goals.

9

Tough Times Don't Last, Tough People Do

Do you have what it takes to make it? Do you have the gumption to look up at Mount Everest and not wince at its enormity?
Do you have the courage to keep going when all others say you
are a fool? Do you have the ability to disregard reality and all
the dreams that it has destroyed? Do you have the patience to
realize that even though you may have worked your tail off the
last few years, you are still three to five years away from making
or launching your idea? Do you have the ability to live with
failure? Lastly and most importantly, do you have what it takes
to rise each and everyday, look yourself in the mirror and say "I
will not rest until I have accomplished what I set out to do?" If

you answered yes to all of these questions, then I truly believe you have what it takes to be successful.

If you want something, then go get it. It will not be easy, and it demands great strength of character. If you have dreams and ambitions, then you owe it to yourself to see them through. Go for it; after all we only live once. After graduate school I realized just how hard things would be in the real world. I also began to wonder what makes someone like Bill Gates or Steve Jobs different from the rest of us? What do they possess that we do not? Obviously, they are extremely intelligent individuals. Other successful individuals may be of average intelligence, but they seem to have made it big. What has been the key to their success? Perhaps we will never know why certain individuals make it and many do not.

My philosophy has been that in order to enact my ideas and dreams, things will be hard, and that is okay. I accept the fact that dreams are not often easy to achieve; they are meant to be a challenge. It is that same challenge that is what makes them special and separates them from the rest of life. Often in life anything that is easy to enact might not be special, but dreams are special and they should be treated as just that. They should be treated as sacred because, for many of us, they are what keep us going day in and day out.

YOU HAVE A COLLEGE DEGREE, NOW WHAT?

I am a firm believer in life that it is best to have a short term memory. Too many people linger on past mistakes and failures. The best attitude to take is to forget quickly. Forgetting quickly does not necessarily have to mean that learning is not taking place. It simply means that a certain individual will not sit and dwell on the past. Dwelling on the past is not an effective strategy at all. It leads to nowhere and promotes a negative image.

Throughout my life I have always played and had a great passion for the game of golf. Early on when I started playing golf, I would let one bad hole ruin my entire day. I realized that dwelling on that one hole would most likely make me play the next few holes very terribly. I decided the best attitude that I could take would be to instantly shake off the previous bad hole and start fresh. This approach in life is definitely worth trying.

Having a short-term memory is one of the single greatest attributes successful persons can possess. It means that negative results will not stop them in their pursuit. This has been a philosophy that I have tried to live out each day. There is no point in lingering on the past. If you receive a bad grade on a test, there is no reason to sit and dwell on that bad grade. Examine what exactly went wrong and how you can go about it differently to achieve a different result next time. Successful people do not dwell on situations they cannot control. No one can control the past, so there is no point in wasting precious time and energy on it. Focus on how past mistakes can make a better future.

Several of my colleagues from graduate school have had situations where job promotions have not gone in their favor. They were down and depressed for weeks. It was, therefore, my responsibility at this time to help them get out of these dark and low places. It is important to remember that we can all control our mental frame of mind. If we want to put ourselves in a dark and low place, we have the power to do so. On the other end of the spectrum, if we want to put ourselves in a positive and motivated place, we have the power to do so as well. We can determine where exactly we want to be mentally, and that same mental approach is one of the most important approaches that we can possess as humans.

Having a short-term memory is extremely important to maintaining a positive attitude. I have seen many of my colleagues reflect a negative attitude by the expression on their faces. Perhaps they were constantly harkening back to all the bad job experiences they previously had. I saw many of these individuals with the same negative faces as they walked into new job interviews, faces that showed mental scars and a tired outlook on life. If you do not have a short-term memory, it can eventually have an effect on your personal brand.

My own short-term memory has allowed me to create and maintain a fresh outlook on life and my own situation. In the past I would be very negative and down on myself when I would contact certain individuals and never be able to get a response back. It was most disturbing when I knew I aced a job interview but failed to secure the job. These times were extremely frustrating for me, but once again there is no point in becoming negative. Implementing this philosophy has led me to possess a good state of mind and a strong body. Once you start having the attitude that things from the past are just that, things from the past, you will begin to feel better in both body and spirit. Being both mentally and physically fit is one of the most crucial components to success. It is important that both are in complete harmony and balance with one another. One fact remains extremely clear; I am at my best when my mind and body are working together, and I maintain a short-term memory. There simply is no substitute for this kind of thinking.

~

I cannot tell you how many times I have felt like throwing in the towel or, in my case, the keyboard. I have had those days where it just seemed as if everything was impossible. There have been days when I just wanted to walk out on the job. It seemed as if the more people made mistakes, the more they were rewarded. This is often how it seems to work. The ones who work hard receive very little for their work while the ones who constantly break all the rules and get into trouble frequently get all the breaks. It is important not to look at it from this viewpoint because frustration will only kick in.

The question that I would ask anyone is why in the world he or she would want to give up and quit. Do you seriously think that by quitting, someone is going to magically come and take you by the hand and lead you to success? We have to be our own biggest supporters because sometimes we may be the only supporter that we have. For many, quitting is just a reality, a way of life if you may have it. I never viewed quitting as an option; I just saw it as nothing. I refuse to recognize that the word quit even exists in the English language.

This was a helpful hint that allowed me to get through the tough and desperate times that we all feel now and again. To this day I despise the word quit. I think that if the word had never been invented, people would not quit because they would not know what it means to quit. The best way to remove this word from your vocabulary is to simply keep going, and no matter what happens, to rise in the morning ready to embark upon your journey. Each day should be a journey, and that is one of the great things about life. If you mess up one day, you always have tomorrow to start over.

Tomorrow is the key to it all. Tomorrow brings new challenges and new opportunities to succeed. In the world of sales, tomorrow is always the most important. Having been in sales myself for a short period of time, I know that it is how one follows up a good day that counts. One could sell thousands of dollars the first day, yet the next day that person has no guarantee of duplicating the same results. The real key to success is to not rest on your laurels and to always remain hungry and motivated. Every time I achieved something, I was always asking myself how I could take my expertise to the next level.

Remaining hungry is one of the key ingredients to building an individual with no desire to quit within them. This is the model person that we should strive to be. It is one who may continue to take negative hits and blows, but it is also one who keeps going. That is the key to it all, keep going. When you reach that point where you feel yourself inches away from quitting, find that strength and keep going. You will be glad you did, and you might look on that near moment where you almost quit as a turning point in your life. Quitting is extremely easy, but continuing up the mountain can, at times, be a daunting task. Only those who are mentally strong and fit can endure the challenges that the mountain will present. The mountain will get the best of most people, but every once in awhile you will find someone who simply refuses to give up. Be that individual, and do not give up at any cost.

I cannot emphasize enough about believing in yourself, for you may soon realize that your inner strength is the only supporter in your corner of the ring. How do you keep going? How do you fight the urge to quit? One solution I have found is through the correct mental approach. I have taken it upon myself to be the most stubborn person on the face of the earth. I invite all to laugh at me and my ideas for I do not view this negatively. I allow this to serve as a positive motivation toward success. The voices of people who have laughed at me continually ring in my head, and I will not rest until the ringing of these voices goes away. The only way to make the laughter go away will be to turn my ideas into a reality.

So many people like to laugh at and put down others. These are what some have called "the idea killers." They are quick to shoot down ideas as if they themselves have tried them. Do not listen to such individuals. We constantly hear on television the so-called experts critiquing who will win the big sporting events. They say this team is going to win or that team will not win. If they truly were so-called experts, then they would be retired on the beach, for they would have been able to bet everything on the big game and won. Why then do we take advice from people who are not experts and may not even be aware of the given field that we are discussing? These people's negative comments should be dismissed as simply that, nothing more, nothing less.

I have heard it enough in my own life. Many take it upon themselves to make comments about and criticize others, yet they never even take into context how that certain individual feels. The bottom line is that many pretend to be critics, yet have no knowledge or expertise to back up their arguments. Their arguments are often based on little or no research, yet many people routinely listen to their advice. You must listen to yourself. You should make the decisions in your life, and let no one, and I repeat no one, get in your way. Once you have this mind-set in place, you will be that much closer to succeeding and reaching your goals.

~

Many people with whom we associate could possibly be considered a negative force of energy. Many negative individuals do not want people to be motivated or to be successful, for they themselves do not possess these characteristics. They do not have ambition and heart to achieve greatness, so they want to see others just as they are. Be wary of these people and where you may encounter them. You most undoubtedly have a few of these people working with you. They are everywhere, and they have given up. For whatever reason they simply called it quits a long time ago and threw in the towel. Once I routinely encountered these individuals, it only made me work harder to not be like them. I realized who they were and what they were all about. Individuals such as these often appear to be waiting for someone to hand them an opportunity. Most opportunities do not fall from the sky, and once you realize this you will be closer to achieving your own goals and dreams. Opportunities are created, for the most part, and successful determined people know this.

Obstacles and negative energy can come from many different sources. They are both frustrating and time-consuming to overcome. Negative sources of energy can range from bad habits to individuals that we regularly encounter each day. They both have a negative effect on us, and it should be our job to do our best to eliminate all negative aspects of our lives. Eliminating these negative aspects is not an easy task at all.

Understand what exactly is working against you. What is it that may be prohibiting you from reaching your goals? Is it lack of time, lack of resources, or simply lack of interest? Whatever the answer might be, it is important that we all determine what it is and then work to change the outcome. It is crucial to remember that you have the power to affect your life positively or negatively. You control your destiny, and you can also control your own demise.

Work hard to achieve great things. Realize that everything is constantly working against us. Once these realizations are, in fact, made, it will make success that much more possible. One must first examine his or her weaknesses and then build on them until they are no longer weaknesses. The real sign of a champion is the realization of weaknesses and flaws. Individuals who believe they have no flaws are in for a great awakening experience. We all have weaknesses about us upon which we can improve. I like to think of my weaknesses the same way I treat reading and learning. The more I read, the more I realize how much I do not know, and the more I work on my weaknesses, the more weaknesses I realize I have.

Pinpoint your negative flaws, and work on them until they are no longer negative flaws. It is impossible to believe that an individual can eliminate all flaws, but it is possible to eliminate enough flaws so that you have less than your competitors. This is the best way to become the complete package.

~

As I slowly moved into the work world with my college degrees, I began to learn lessons that I would take with me for the rest of my life. The ability to be persistent and relentless is a combination for success. I took the attitude that I would be the most persistent person in the world and let it be known that no matter how many times I was shot down for potential opportunities, I would be back again. It is an empowering feeling to know that you will stop at nothing. I encourage everyone to be the most stubborn person on the face of the earth, and do not let others determine what you are capable of accomplishing.

One aspect that has appeared to hurt individuals has been the part of their lives when they simply hit the aptly entitled "wall." This is where individuals will work as hard as they possibly can, take a step back, and realize that they have gotten nowhere. My advice would be the same for an individual who has maxed out in the gym while bench pressing. He or she seems to build weight each and every month, and then that person hits a roadblock where it is impossible to bench press anymore. You must find the inner strength to not give in. It is easy to quit, and I have felt that way many times myself. You have to convince yourself that quitting is not an option.

Many have said that the difference between success and failure is oftentimes so small that it cannot be measured. What is it that separates the truly great individuals from the ordinary? What is it that they possess that has allowed them to achieve feats deemed impossible? Some would say it is money and knowing the correct people. This may be true because having money or coming from money does make certain things easier. I would look to the other side of why certain individuals have achieved monumental levels of success. I look at it from the standpoint that they decided to keep going while others quit. You must have the determination and knowledge to keep going even when it seems as if things will never change. I am a firm believer that we decide when it is over.

Deciding when something is over can be the difference between success or failure. Oftentimes in life we set deadlines for ourselves. We tell ourselves that if we do not achieve something by a certain age, then we will give up. Why would anyone want to act like this anyway? This means that if one follows this philosophy, life has been turned into one big timetable. I do not like the idea of a timetable because it reduces everything to a schedule. Time should not be the sole determining factor for setting goals. We should make our determinations on what we can accomplish based on how we feel and not how old we are. Many people have taken longer than others to find success, and some have found it very early.

Successful people strive for success rather than just achieving results by a certain age. My own instincts will tell me when it is time to stop trying. So far, I have heard no voices from within me telling me to quit, so what results is that you have a person who is beyond motivated. I would encourage you to do the same and not give in. Giving in because you are a certain age does not make much sense. I will pull the plug on my dreams when I decide it is time to pull the plug, and that is the way it is going to be.

One of the greatest attributes that a successful person can possess is the desire to keep going against all odds. Very few carry this belief and attitude within them. There have been many times when I have felt like sitting down and quitting, but I did not because I knew it was not time to do so. I guess it is fair to say that I was listening to that little voice that exists within all of us. This little voice is saying different statements to every-one. Some individuals may constantly hear a voice expressing the belief that they cannot accomplish their dreams or the goals that they have set out to accomplish. My own voice has always expressed the belief that I can do it. Time and time again, I have constantly heard, "Keep going, you can do it." These words and statements may sound classic, cliché and down right cheesy, but at your lowest point they just might turn out to be your saving grace when you hit that "wall."

When everyone believes that you cannot accomplish something, to what will you turn? Who will be there to serve as motivation and that guiding hand that will give you the extra nudge you need to succeed? You just may find one day that if you do reach the stage where all are of the opinion that you can-not achieve a certain goal, that inner voice may simply be worth its weight in gold.

By the law of numbers, there will be a certain amount of people in the world who quit and give up. We are surrounded by them each and everyday we exist. They come in all shapes and sizes. These individuals are waiting for a free lunch or someone to provide them with the magical opportunity that will change their lives forever. Do not be one of these individuals.

The issue of giving in will affect all of us throughout our lives, no matter what we find ourselves doing or attempting. The key is to not give in. It is this philosophy that will, hopefully, help individuals to feel as if they can accomplish whatever they want, and I live this to the fullest. I firmly intend to follow my heart as well as the morals and beliefs to which I hold true. It is up to each individual to find out in what he or she firmly believes, and I suggest once you do find it, hold on to it until the very end. Once this is attained, success is only a matter of time.

10

Now What?

There are certain individuals who are waiting for perfect and ideal conditions in order to start. This can be applied to many different areas of life. The problem is that the longer you wait, the more you realize there will never be a perfect time because there will always be something in the way. A classic example that I saw with people whom I knew revolved around something as simple as reading a book. After reading an excellent book, I would often recommend it to close friends and colleagues. I would even go as far as to lend them my copy, meaning all they had to do was sit down and read it. This proved too hard for certain individuals as three weeks after giving someone a book, I would always ask what they thought about the book? Most often the reply was that they had not yet found the time to read it. I would first react with a sense of disappointment, and then I would proceed to ask for the book back. I could make better use of the book by going over and reviewing my notes rather than giving it to someone who had no intention of ever reading it.

These individuals are what are called procrastinators. They will never find the time because by putting off something as simple as reading a book to improve their own personal knowledge, they were putting off their lives. These individuals will, most likely, never achieve anything because they will not take the time to do so.

Many people do not realize that the reason why a great number of successful people are where they are today is not by chance but because they took the time to take the steps necessary to get to where they wanted to be. My approach would be that if an individual wants to be a go-getter and make opportunities happen, all he or she simply has to do is to know the difference between a go-getter and a procrastinator. Then that individual needs to dedicate himself or herself to being a go-getter. The more I saw individuals with whom I was acquainted drinking, partying, and wasting both time and money on their ways, I realized that all I had to do was dedicate myself to being the polar opposite of them. As I continued to see individuals whom I would characterize negatively, I desperately wanted to work hard so that I would always be the opposite of them and never let negative behavior stand in the way of my success. I aimed to be a positive individual. Be a breath of fresh air in an overcrowded and dense world. I am not stating that these individuals are bad people, but they are not ones I would use as role models for myself.

Oftentimes people would say that I thought I was better than they were. I have never thought this about myself. I believe I can be more capable than these individuals and I expect more of myself. I never foresaw this as happening because this is something with which I always struggled. For a long time I always thought as if I should be out doing what other individuals my own age were doing instead of studying and working on business plans for companies that did not even exist yet. Certain friends of mine would tell me "You should be coming out with us," yet I never listened.

If I was not going to listen to friends, then why should I care if so-called experts said I could not launch a certain business. Why should I care if a corporate executive did not believe my business model would work in the real world? I have never listened to anyone except myself. Most people are stopped dead in their tracks because they heed everyone else's warning. It is important to let the world know that you will stop at nothing to achieve your goals.

YOU HAVE A COLLEGE DEGREE, NOW WHAT?

I remember back to an informational interview that I once had with one of the most well-respected athletic directors in the country. I met with him to determine if he thought that earning a doctorate degree would help my chances of one day ascending to the seat of athletic director. He sat back in his seat and laughed for quite a while and said "You don't want to earn a doctorate degree and be unemployed. You do know that there are only one hundred seventeen Division IA Athletic Directors in the country." This was a moment upon which I often reflect and that serves as great motivation. Business-wise I would like nothing more than to prove this individual wrong. For anyone reading this, it is time to think back to a superior who may have discouraged you from trying to achieve something, and then continue until you simply prove them wrong. The time to achieve your dreams is now.

~

Success in life all boils down to keeping the momentum going. The momentum refers to the number of activities an individual has going on at once. The more ideas and projects I had revolving, the luckier I came to be. Some people would say that a good professional gofer is the luckiest golfer on the face of the earth as he or she routinely gets good break after good break. What those individuals fail to realize is that he is also one of the hardest workers on the planet. Luck comes from consistently putting yourself in exactly the same position. Great professional golfers consistently put themselves in position to win, and, consequently, it appears to be luck. It is not luck. The same can go for business. The more you repeatedly put yourself in someone's face, the more likely you are to find success.

Oftentimes I would feel as if my momentum were coming to a screeching halt. Keeping it going is all about refusing to stop. I simply refused to give up. When I felt as if my momentum was coming to a halt, I would do all in my power to make sure that I was meeting with people in my respective industries. Many individuals will lose their momentum and do nothing to get it back. Without it we are stuck in the quagmire of life, slowly sinking to the bottom.

Getting one's momentum back can be as simple as setting up important meetings with people in your industry. This is an easy way to get back into the swing of things, but so few people do this. It baffles me that people sit around and wait for opportunities to fall their way. I always operated on the principle that opportunities of a lifetime do not fall from the sky onto your lap. There are a few rare occasions where this notion might be true, but, for the most part, it is an accurate statement. I always prided myself on the fact that I fully intended to be responsible for the opportunities that came my way. With this sense of mind, I felt as if I were the one in control of my future.

I would not wait for opportunities to come my way; I would go in search of them.

~

I know from experience that upon completion of their college degrees, many of my colleagues were frustrated by their situations. They were frustrated for a multitude of reasons. One of my own beliefs is that I feel many people think that once they have completed their college degrees, jobs and opportunities should be lining up at the door. This was not the case as neither my colleagues nor I had a job lined up after graduation. This can be very deflating after years of hard work. You would think that one would be rewarded after having completed an advanced degree, but this was not true. Many colleagues of mine had to go back to working for free.

One thing I learned from earning my college degrees was that they entitled me to nothing. What they did entitle me to was the invitation to begin to learn further. I had been invited by myself and my interests to read and learn all that I could. All that I would eventually learn would begin to help me in the future.

Earning my college degrees was a very humbling experience. In fact, it often appears that young people may be at a severe disadvantage with a college degree because they may have more education than the people who are trying to hire them. In this case those individuals may be intimidated by a person with such a degree.

There may also exist a sort of arrogance and jealousy amongst others who do not possess such college degrees. They often like to put down those who do. I would often get harassed if I was not able to figure something out. "Come on, Mr. Master's Degree," was a routine statement that I would begin to hear and still bothers me yet to this day. Just because someone possesses a bachelor's or master's degree does not mean that they know everything. Individuals who make these statements are most likely not very well read because they would realize that the more one reads and learns, the more one realizes how much is not known. A college degree, in some sense, exposes your weaknesses to how much you do not know. I have felt for quite some time now that I am on a quest, and no one can help me. I have to make this quest for knowledge by myself, and I encourage you to do the same. Learn all that you can, for with that knowledge comes the opportunity to follow your dreams.

~

It is important to sometimes take a step back and examine the trends that are taking place in your life. Sometimes we are so wrapped up and enthralled in our own lives that we cannot see exactly what is and what is not working. It is necessary for all of us to take a look at ourselves, from time to time, to see what we can do to improve. This often is the only way to examine what we might be doing wrong. Numerous times I have received helpful hints from people because it is easier for another person to see what is taking place when that person is not actively involved in what you are doing. Helpful advice can be offered by anyone. It simply does not matter. What does matter is that trends are examined.

Oftentimes it seems that some people would be failing when using a certain strategy or technique. Despite this they would still continue on with the exact same approach. It is as if they are magically hoping that their strategy would eventually prove to be successful.

When I begin to slump with my golf game, I do not continue on with my current strategy. I will usually take a step back, examine where I need my swing to be, and how I will get my swing there. Once all that is complete, I will find success. I learned early on that strategy is important. You can have an excellent business model in place, but it is how you execute it that counts and matters most. Execution is key anywhere. In golf it is how you execute your golf swing that matters most. If you do not execute it correctly, it is very likely that you will not find success.

Some people go through life using the same strategy from time-to-time. They do not meet their goals and objectives, yet despite this they never change their overall strategy. I have met many individuals like this, and I also have been guilty of these actions. I would find myself trying the same method over and over, expecting magically that the result would all of the sudden be different. Sometimes in life we are so entrenched in what we are doing that we fail to see exactly what we are doing. This can be solved by taking a step back and examining yourself from the outside. Take a step outside of your body and observe yourself. Are you going about things the correct way? Could you possibly enact another philosophy to get the results you desire? These are the questions that one should be asking of oneself.

~

I feel that there are two routes to take in life. The first route is that you become just another member of society and you read about history. The second route is to go out and make history. I choose the second route, and I hope you will, too. It is important to realize that the second route will not be easy, and there will be people trying to bring you down all the time. Much like Nile crocodiles waiting in the rivers of Africa to pull down unsuspecting wilderbeast, the same can be said for life. Some people want to see others fall and be dragged down because it makes them feel better about their own situation.

I cannot stress enough how important it is to treat others as you would like to be treated. It is often stated or implied that one must be cutthroat and vicious to make it to the top. I stress a different route and attitude to take. Be helpful to others, teach others, and do not be afraid to be nice to people. Too many individuals feel as if the only way to make it is to be downright mean.

Throughout my working career I have always taken it upon myself to help whomever needed help. It did not matter who it was or with what that person needed help. Do to others and the favor will be returned. So many people make it to the top and forget from where they came. That is a philosophy that only makes the corporate world even more cutthroat. Many who are not willing to help others makes it harder for new people to enter a given field. The fact is that corporate CEO's do not start as CEO's. It is important to remember that no one starts at the top. Everyone has been at the bottom at some time in their life.

There are always exceptions to this, but, for the most part, it is true. Teaching others only serves to make one that much smarter. Teaching is one of the great gifts that we, as humans, can offer to others. Some would even argue that teaching and learning are more valuable than money. Knowledge is freedom, and the more you know, the more you reduce your risks in life.

NOW WHAT?

~

If one compares life to picking fruit from an apple tree, we can all learn a very important lesson. There are many people in life who simply want the easy way out. They are content to stay on the ground and reach for the apples which are on the lowest branches. They have set their sights and goals low, and they will most likely reach them. I would argue for anyone to set their sights on the apples at the very top of the tree. This means to aim so high in life that you have picked a place to which you will ascend that few will ever even entertain reaching.

It is also important to remember that just as there are individuals who will reach for the lowest apples on the tree, there are others who will try and cheat their way to the top of the apple tree. They will cheat their way up the tree, cheating more and more with each branch they climb. I would also urge all who have picked up this book to ascend the tree with integrity. Integrity is something which we should all possess. Some just choose to display it more than others. Acquire the knowledge that will get you to that bright and shiny apple that is sitting all by itself at the top of the tree.

Remember, only you can acquire the knowledge necessary to chase and follow your dreams to the top of the tree. Those who choose to cheat their way to the top are most likely doing so without acquiring the necessary knowledge. They are looking for a ladder in which they can literally steal that lone apple atop the tree.

Knowledge and integrity are two of the greatest things that we as humans possess. I am a firm believer that knowledge and integrity are all that one needs in order to climb to the top of the apple tree. Let others cheat for they have no morals, and, at the end of the day, I truly believe knowledge will surpass lies, cheating, and deception. Set your sights to the highest goals you can, and then while maintaining your integrity, work on acquiring the necessary knowledge in order to get there.

I have always told people that I think my greatest weakness is that I lack experience, and my greatest attribute is that I do not know yet what I am capable of accomplishing. I intend to shoot for the stars. Do not be afraid to shoot for those stars as many people might be. It is only over when we decide it is over. Reality and reason are the voice of the scared and timid individual. I call out to anyone who has ever had a dream to follow it, chase it, and stop at nothing in your pursuit of it.

About the Authors

Michael Esola has worked for prominent organizations that include the Oakland Athletics Baseball organization, the San Jose Sabercats of the Arena Footbal League, and the San Francisco Tennis Club. He earned his Bachelor of Arts and Master of Arts degrees from the University of San Francisco. He is currently working on his second book, and serves as a managing partner with Prehistoric Entertainment and EJ Consulting.

Wesley Jones has worked for prominent organizations that include The Walt Disney Company, Six Flags Theme Parks, and Target Corporation. He earned his Master of Arts and Master of Science degrees from the University of San Francisco. He is currently working on his third book, serves as a managing partner with Prehistoric Entertainment, and serves as an Organization Development and Human Resources consultant for EJ Consulting.

More Information

Is your organization stuck? Need a boost in productivity and morale? Want to ensure that your education and experience are working for you? Visit www.ejconsultingllc.com for creative solutions that can help your organization's most valuable asset succeed...People.